Is the secret to a full, rich life hidden in the "either-or" fate of marital status?

Is the foundation of my fulfillment largely a reflection of how I view myself?

Am I just one big mistake waiting to happen— or am I a unique miracle created in the image of a Father who cares for me as an individual?

This little book will enable you to re-assess your sex and marital status—and to view life from the vantage point of a loving Father's arms.

HOW TO BE **A**

COMPLETE NEW YOU

SINGLE or MARRIED

BY VIRGINIA GOLD APPLE

A Division of G/L Publications
Glendale, California, U.S.A.

In loving appreciation to my family
Life's richest gift to me
Father and Mother
Steve and Karen
Don and Emilie
Who reflect His giving love

The publishers do not necessarily endorse the entire contents
of all publications referred to in this book.

Any omission or error in credits is unintentional.
The publisher requests documentation for future printings.

Scripture verses quoted in text are from
the following versions of the Bible:
KJV—King James Version.
ASV—American Standard Version.
RSV—Revised Standard Version. Copyrighted 1946 and 1952
by the Division of Christian Education of the NCCC in the
U.S.A., and used by permission.
Amplified—The Amplified Bible (Grand Rapids: Zondervan
Publishing House, 1965). Used by permission.
TLB—The Living Bible, Paraphrased (Wheaton: Tyndale House,
Publishers, 1971). Used by permission.
NASB—New American Standard Bible. © The Lockman Foundation,
1971. Used by permission.
Phillips—The New Testament in Modern English, copyright
J.B. Phillips 1958. Used by permission of the Macmillan Company.

Published by
Regal Books Division, G/L Publications
Glendale, California 91209, U.S.A.

Library of Congress Catalog Card No. 74-32321
ISBN 0-8307-0350-0

CONTENTS

INTRODUCTION

I'm weary of the brave attempts of our society, including the Christian community, to boost the "inevitable" sagging spirits of the unfortunate, unfulfilled, unattached, unclaimed blessings. I refer to those of us who presently enjoy the state of "unmatrimony."

When the list of prospective hopefuls ends with Uncle Buzzard's great nephew's half-brother, one consoling approach may be a pious, condescending, "Your sacrifice and suffering will surely be rewarded someday, my dear," while others may intellectually extol the eternal merits of contented celibacy.

At the other end of the spectrum is the super-swinging set, singing its song of freedom, fun and frolics. From Adam's rib to women's lib, that superficial high of the "Symphony to Singles" has been shallow and disappointing. The middle-of-the-roader may vacillate from one mood to another. One day he is courageously dying to self and all earthly desires—the next he is living to "Eat, drink and be merry" for tomorrow I may be convicted to die to self again!

On the other side of the great divide, marital mania is viewed from equally different perspectives. Its mysterious magic promises tremendous recuperative powers from all frustration, emptiness, and pain. The instant-happiness switch is flipped by the cozy couple, supposedly preventing problems or sorrow from dimming its eternal flame.

At a different altitude, others vehemently warn against the monstrous trap, the dread freedom-snatcher, the suburban slave-maker. The less spirited may apathetically agree to swallow the matrimonial pill and live in not-too-peaceful coexistence.

What does God purpose my outlook to be? Is the secret to be a full, rich life hidden in the either-or fate of marital status? I suppose that what I rest upon as the foundation of my fulfillment is largely reflecting just how I view myself. Am I just one big mistake waiting to happen—or am I a unique miracle created in the image of a Father who cares for me as an individual? "Single sighs and marital madness" need never occur if I gain insight into the heart of a sovereign God who desires to give me His best in infinite wisdom and and love.

I'm aware of the multitudes of articles, books and lectures—pep-talks that deal with the subject of achieving the highest quality of life. I find many helpful and encouraging truths from those who have already expressed themselves, and I'm challenged to explore my own thoughts and feelings on the matter. It's easy for me to become stagnantly content with the insights of others instead of searching and discovering my own thrust for living. And too, the majority of writers and popular speakers are, or have been, married.

I desire to speak from another frame of reference, that of a young and unmarried. In later years I will probably reflect back and see the immaturity and lack of foresight in some of my thinking. Yet I believe that this project will be helpful to me, and I hope to others, as I write from *this* moment of life. I'm not looking back in retrospection, but forward to a beautiful, exciting future. Some notes I jotted down a few years ago when reading Psalm 37 seem appropriate to introduce my thoughts.

"Let me be contently involved with the present tense of my life instead of anxiously revolving my energies around the mysterious unknown. That unknown will unfold in time into a beautiful revelation of God's love. That's a thrilling fact of my life based on the very character of my unchanging God."

These pages are not intended to be a verbal tennis match of the pros and cons of the single set versus the yea's and nay's of marriage. Even the term "singleness" is one I dislike for I believe that it conveys a mistaken distinction. In one context, we all qualify as "singles." The basic guidelines for purpose and fulfillment are identical for all of God's children. We are "singles" in His sight all of our lives. I think that the more we grasp this truth, the nearer we will be to a balanced, happy view of life. As we begin to act upon that truth, we will be challenged to begin developing our own God-given potential.

My thinking includes reflections of the disappointments and delights of past and present experiences. They are not unique or profound, but they are mine and I have learned and am learning from them. Naturally they are confined in content to the young unmarried context of my life, but principles may be gathered that are also applicable to the married and to the male. I gladly admit a woman's point of view for blessed reasons beyond my control. (Any male reader thus far may be growling, "Yeah, lady, and ever since Adam we've been listening to women too much!")

I just can't discuss issues touching the core of life without entering the forbidden subject domain of manhood. Life is shared by two distinct categories of Homo sapiens, and one cannot be understood when isolated from the other. So any man is welcome to venture within.

Let's stretch our minds and faith and attempt to reach that highest quality of expectant, fulfilled, joyful living that God has prepared for us, instead of grudgingly compromising as to "who has it the best" between the Ms., Miss, Mrs. and Mr. May we envision all that God longs to provide for us and take hold and claim His promises, in Christ Jesus.

———————————————

"He that spared not his own Son, but delivered him up for us all, how shall he not with him also freely give us all things" (Rom. 8:32, *KJV*).

5

ONE
HOW TO BE SINGLE WITHOUT REALLY TRYING

"You're pretty religious, aren't you, Virginia?" This unexpected question sailed in out of the blue during a cram session for nursing finals. My agnostic friend flashed a look of confused surprise as I answered somewhat teasingly a simple, "No."

"But you read your Bible and are forever going to some church," she protested.

I smiled as I explained, "Yes, I guess that could label me as 'religious' but that sounds so cold and formal. My focus is not on some man-made ecclesiastical tradition. The most important thing in my life, the very *why* of my whole existence, is my relationship to a personal God."

We continued into a lively discussion, never to return to the essentials of cardio-vascular surgery. The "heart issues" that were explored that evening had infinitely greater significance.

Dead-End Street, Really Dead
An enthusiastic young militant once asked me to sign a petition to bless, or ban (I forget which) some virtuous cause. I made the mistake of asking *Why?*

After several minutes of "go get 'em" jargon with no hint of rationality, she ended with a weak, "Well, it sounds good anyway!"

In our present age, very little is definite in content or meaning. Relativism has grasped our minds and often prevents a sense of certainty about anything. To march, strike or sit may be simple; to know why is another matter.

Even within the world's religious structure we are told to take the great leap of faith into an experiential puddle we happen upon. After all, say some existentialists, God isn't Someone. He is just a nebulous sensation to tingle our senses. However, this mental suspension into nothingness is much more than intellectual irrationality. Trying to juggle that good religious feeling with an "anything goes" life-style is quite a feat. For, when the vise of life tightens, if there's no objective foundation to resist the crunch, the pieces are not often easy to put together again.

We lack a sense of "why" because we lack an objective authority in life. A gal from the love-bead era came to me after I had spoken to a high school group about Christ and responded earnestly, "Look, what you have is beautiful . . . what I have is beautiful too. Let's just both do our own thing."

I gently inquired, "Just one question, who is your authority?"

Startled, she stammered, "Well, I don't guess I have one."

"Yes you do," I replied. "You are your own authority. But what happens when you come against something you just can't handle?"

After a pause with bowed head she asked, "And your authority is God?"

"Yes, but not just how I imagine Him to be. My authority is God as He has revealed Himself in His Word, the Bible, a written, objective authority," I explained.

Doing your own thing gets old, especially when the reflection in your mirror is someone you don't like and really don't even know. The road of life, liberty and happiness often becomes a freeway to death, slavery and despair.

Our Grotesque Gods

The great philosophical *why* can never be answered apart from the One who is the Creator and Sustainer of life. He is completely self-existent, self-sufficient, transcendent, infinite and totally incomprehensible. Yet, in our religious thinking, we continue to mold Him into a concept that is completely other—a weak god after our own image. We envision Him as a kindly old grandfather, too sentimental and weak of spirit to scold or punish. We would like an understandable god, one we could manipulate at our own convenience.

This weak substitute is hardly greater than the attempts of the Greeks and Romans in their mythology. We are perhaps too sophisticated to picture our deity as half-man, half-beast, but the creation of our deceitful hearts is just as hideous, erroneous and blasphemous to a holy God.

A.W. Tozer in his book, *The Knowledge of the Holy*, writes:

"Our real idea of God may lie buried under the rubbish of conventional religious notions and may require an intelligent and vigorous search before it is finally unearthed and exposed for what it is. A god begotten in the shadows of a fallen heart will quite naturally be no true likeness to a true God. What comes into our minds when we think about God is the most important thing about us. It is impossible to keep our moral practices sound and our inward attitudes right while our idea of God is erroneous or inadequate."[1]

Majesty or Mutation?

What we need is to discover the meaning of Proverbs 9:10, "The fear of the Lord is the beginning of wisdom." A true vision of the greatness and majesty of God can only result in this awesome respect and worship. This fear is not one that binds and cripples but is, instead, a solid spirit-set that is gloriously freeing. "Ye shall know the truth, and the truth shall make you free" (John 8:32). As we see and worship God as He is, we begin to find our own significance and a new freedom to see life differently. God in all His glory and power, willed that man, through his own choice, could come into a special relationship with Him. It's a relationship at which even the angels marvel.

Help me understand the meaning of your gifts to me, Lord.

Not only your complete pardon for my rebellion but another position that I cannot grasp—

Daughter of the King

Heir of God

Joint-heir with Christ

Inheritor of all riches in infinite glory

May I please the heart of my heavenly Father

As I claim the spirit of adoption

9

Whereby I cry, Abba Father. (Based on Rom. 8:15-17.)

Our behavior rarely resembles what one would expect from majesty—sons and daughters of the King. We show more similarity to multiple mutations of the monkey. Our so-called evolutionary ascent from beast to beauty doesn't do a thing for my identity crisis. I'd much rather claim restoration back into God's family and original intent than to live in fear that my species may take a sudden turn for the worse.

Love Story

"I will be like God," boasted the angel of light in rebellion—for which God stripped him of his heavenly status and cast him from His presence. "I will be like God, to know good and evil," said Adam and Eve as they violated God's only limitation in a world they dominated and freely enjoyed.

This rebellious spirit of disobedience and independence is the essence of man's condition today, just as it was for Lucifer and the first created beings on earth. We can gaze quietly within ourselves and see the same stubborn resistance and disobedient spirit. "I will be my own authority . . . no one tells me how to run my life." How we must grieve the Father-heart of God who longs to give us every blessing, every promise that He created us to be and have. This is our basic problem—a yawning chasm between God and man, hewn by man's choice to rebel. But God acted to bridge that gap. And it all begins with His heart of love.

We hear much about love, whether it be a heart

flutter, a liver shiver, or a brain pain. The "real thing" is hard to unearth from beneath the sentimentality and gush. Very little is known about the meat and backbone of love, although the whole world bow before the skeleton of lust. The verse "God is love" (1 John 4:16) sends us to the Source for a definition.

An instant replay of Genesis 1—3 is again helpful in our understanding. God, motivated by love, brought mankind into the world to enjoy it with all the riches He longed to bestow. His quality of love, not based on any need within Himself, sought to give—in unimagined abundance. For man to return God's love it was necessary for him to have freedom of will to choose. This freedom to choose is the very breath at the heart of love.

During one of my dateless periods I was miserably enjoying my warm pit of self-pity, bemoaning my fate in "Nobody-loves-me" syllables. My sweet, patient mom gave me a sincere, "But you know that your father and I love you, very much."

Not the least bit consoled I replied, "But, Mother, you and Daddy *have* to love me! I want someone to choose to just because he *wants* to!"

Of course, I realize that my parents love me by choice and I'm continually overwhelmed with the unselfish quality of their love. An act of will initiates love and a divine quality of love continues to choose only what is right and best for the beloved. God demonstrated this to the first man and woman and He gave them the free option to respond. But, man chose his own selfish way and continues to do so today.

Within the mystery of the Godhead, at the birth of creation, an infinite fountain of love planned grace for the rebellious man. God continued to show His giving quality of love by invading history in the form of a man. Jesus lived for us, knowing all our earthbound problems, yet without sin (Heb. 4:15). He died for us, taking upon Himself the filth of our wickedness, and suffered the punishment that should have been ours.

He did that for us as individuals, as if each of us was the only person in all of history. The incarnation, life, and death of this God-man is such a miracle of love. The Resurrection, a culmination of victory over sin and its results, gives us power to live again in unbroken love and fellowship with our Creator.

One Great Imperative

There is only one great imperative in life—the restoration of our relationship with God. We can choose to repent of our rebellion and receive forgiveness, submitting ourselves to God's authority. It is this which gives us new life, quite literally, to discover and reach God's highest for us. Without it, the task of knowing fulfillment is ridiculously impossible.

These facts are hardly new revelations to the majority of us, I suppose. But gather them together and we'll have our first and absolute requisite step toward happy, successful living: repent, receive, submit. We must first plant our feet on the solid foundation of God's authority. Then we can discover the secrets of satisfaction. Then we can discuss the unmarried or the married life—for we shall know the meaning of life. Only here can we begin to see a true vision of who God is as He enlightens us. Only here will the tumult of meaninglessness be stilled and the "God-shaped vacuum" in every heart be filled. Only in His mighty arms can we first discover the experience of true, everlasting love.

If God is your authentic authority, let's worship Him together. If not, your response to His love in repentance and submission can make Him your authority. The new position of "heir of God, and joint-heir with Christ" can be yours. The *why* of life can be answered with a certainty that nothing can shake.

"For I am convinced that nothing can ever separate us from his love. Death can't, and life can't. The angels won't, and all the powers of hell itself cannot keep God's love away. Our fears for today, our worries about tomorrow, or where we are—high above the sky, or in the deepest ocean—nothing will ever be able to separate us from the love of God demonstrated by our Lord Jesus Christ when he died for us" (Rom. 8:38,39, *TLB*).

I'll never forget the wonderful privilege of watching God draw one of my friends to Himself. A Phi Beta Kappa, magna cum laude graduate from the university, she knelt in the early morning hours and prayed simply, "Lord, I don't understand it all. I just know that I want You." She left later with a new "why," a new Lord, and a sense of inseparable love.

Special Us

We now see ourselves as highly significant individuals, "singles," each one unique in the eyes of a loving God. Our redemption gives us authority and purpose. However, many of us still sing with Eliza Doolittle in "My Fair Lady" some variation of "Wouldn't It Be Loverly." We hold our periodic sigh meetings, yearning for a better life starting with a different us. The transformation that God has in mind for us is far greater than it was for Eliza—from gutter to queenly hall.

13

How exciting it was when I first discovered that God called me, "My Rare Lady" from the moment of my conception. He was preparing wonderful things for me long before I turned from self-direction to Him.

"You made all the delicate, inner parts of my body, and knit them together in my mother's womb. Thank you for making me so wonderfully complex! It is amazing to think about. Your workmanship is marvelous—and how well I know it. You were there while I was being formed in utter seclusion! You saw me before I was born and scheduled each day of my life before I began to breathe. Everyday was recorded in your Book!" (Ps. 139:13-16, *TLB*).

We are significant as individuals because of God's redemptive love and because He fashioned each of us to be a unique masterpiece of divine art. What a tragedy that the majority of us, highly specialized creations, spend most of our waking hours striving to conform to society's mold.

We are robots of *Redbook* and puppets of *Playboy*, spending small fortunes in time, money and effort to look and act like everyone else. And it does take effort to conform . . . . What a grueling circus! By the time I figure out what's "in" and how to get there, the roller coaster makes a ninety-degree turn that leaves me half in, half out, too dizzy to worry about the dip up ahead.

God has better things in store for us.

"Don't copy the behavior and customs of this world, but be a new and different person with a fresh newness in all you do and think. Then you will learn from your own experience how his ways will really satisfy you" (Rom. 12:2, *TLB*).

Just as infinite variety is seen in snowflakes, or in the plant and animal kingdoms, so God has fashioned a tremendous gamut of human variability. Each of us has his own brand of peculiar looks, accentuated by different personalities and temperaments. Some of us drag along at a slow 45 RPM's, while others are whirling at 75 RPM's. Some have their own public address system and don't mind being heard, while others prefer a quieter classified ad approach. Our looks, pace, patterns of expression and other tendencies are all under His creative sovereignty. I like to imagine us as specially designed musical instruments:

May I see each day an opportunity for the
Master Musician to play His Symphony
through this unique instrument.

May I not resist His desire to perfect His
workmanship to bring forth purer melodies.

May I be fashioned into a smooth channel
through which unaltered heavenly notes flow,
as a flute plays as breath gives it life.

May I not despise the drums and cymbals
of His orchestra,
Nor envy the trumpets or violins.

They are His craftsmanship also,
designed for different purposes.

May I learn to appreciate,
to genuinely love them
not striving to be like them
nor trying to change them.

15

May we blend our voices to praise
and worship You, Lord

Our Craftsman, our Composer, our Conductor.

Flight to Freedom

In my teen years, I so wanted to be a lovely harp, graceful and delicate. I found myself more the tuba-type. With 50 percent more leg than I could handle and a short circuit between brain and feet, stairs and curbs for me were meant to be tripped up or down on a near-daily basis. One fellow friend lovingly sent me an original valentine addressed, "To my favorite Ox"!

Another illustration of my charm is set in a lovely wooded park, on a beautiful April afternoon. My date is tenderly pushing my swing as I perch laughingly in the breeze, fresh cotton dress afluttering. I decide to delicately leap off the swing just about the time he gives another substantial push. Blast-off! The first woman astronaut is born. Flying through the air with less than the greatest of ease, I landed crumpled in a casually chosen mud puddle. Cute.

A congenital anomaly, "foot in mouth," added to my talents an unstrung tongue. I was forever saying too much to the wrong people at the wrong time or variations within. Adolescent crisis really hit when Mr. All-American arrived, four inches shorter than I!

I smile now, but remember vividly what a struggle it was for me to thank God for the way He had fashioned me. I saw clearly that if I resented His handiwork in me I would be reluctant to wholly trust Him with the rest of my life. Believing there was a "goof" in my beginnings, how could I be assured that another divine mistake wouldn't occur again.

But, God gives us grace to recognize His goodness so I became convinced of His perfect wisdom in making me. I appreciate my height, laugh at my blunders and take a genuine interest in others instead of centering my concern on myself. The process of "being free to be me" still goes on, and it's exciting!

I realize that my problems are minor compared to really serious handicaps and disabilities. Yet God's goodness is the same for all and self-acceptance is an act of faith and thanksgiving. Its lack can retard spiritual growth and destroy any sense of fulfillment, causing depression and defeat. In *Ms. Means Myself*, Gladys Hunt beautifully explores the subject of self-acceptance:

"I am not talking about egotistic self-love. I am talking about the kind of self-acceptance that affirms our personal worth and frees us from the prison of self-absorption. What is such a woman (and may I add, such a man) free to do? She is free to love God. She is free to love others. Appreciating that God took the initiative in individual lives, she is free to follow His example. She reaches out to others on the basis of love, not need. She is free to forgive because she knows herself forgiven. She accepts herself because God has accepted her."[2]

The image we see of ourselves may be distorted as it was for the elderly gent who saw himself in a store's convex mirror and didn't like the suspicious looking character he saw. The problem of our self-image may exist in the warped surface of our standard. Are we measuring ourselves by society's yardstick or even a godly person's life-style? The problem may also be in our vision, dimmed by resentment and bitterness at our Maker. The distorted reflection of ourselves may be suspicious looking indeed!

God has created and redeemed you. He knows you better than you know yourself. He has purposed a rich life for you, not only in a general sense "to glorify and enjoy Him forever," but with an added dimension. Each one of us is a unique miracle of His, custom-made for a custom-fit life.

God loves us as "singles" and plans to restore our position as His heirs. His creative sovereignty assures us that there were no mistakes in our beginnings. How foolish to reject His master plan—to worry, fret and complain about the loneliness of unmarried life or the trap of wedded existence. What a privilege to live in daily communication with our Master Planner, participating in the perfecting of His work in us. "I am confident of this: that the One who has begun His good work in you will go on developing it until the day of Jesus Christ" (Phil. 1:6, *Phillips*).

Now, what is *our* part in developing our God-given potential? What goals should we set to reach the highest potential? What goals should we set to reach the highest quality of abundant living He has planned for us? God has given me new life. Should my goal be to "go ye and tell others"? God has also given me the beautiful gift of womanhood. Should my goal be living to fulfill my womanhood?

Not exactly . . . .

Footnotes

1. A.W. Tozer, *The Knowledge of the Holy* (New York: Harper & Row Publishers, 1961), pages 9-11.
2. Gladys Hunt, *Ms. Means Myself* (Grand Rapids, Michigan: Zondervan Publishing House, 1972), pages 21,23.

TWO
ONE-TRACK LIFE

Modern living reminds me of a fenced puppy madly rushing to go nowhere. With the absence of meaning in this life and no sense of destiny in the life beyond, we use activity to stuff the void. As believers, we sing of the "sweet by and by" and wistfully sigh for it here and now. We may see a dim glimmer of the golden glow of our promised final destination, but heaven is just too far away to be taken too seriously.

We are like the little fellow who responded with a decisive "No!" when his amazed teacher asked him if he wanted to go to heaven.

"But son, don't you want to be with Jesus when you die?" she urged.

"Oh sure," he replied, "I just thought you were trying to get up a load to go now."

There are times, however, when many of us would gladly hop the daily heavenly express if given a chance, too weary to struggle with this world's woes another day.

19

Not "Where," But "Who"

It is right and good for us to look forward to the place that God has prepared for us. The outer limits of our finite imaginations cannot begin to conceive the wonder of what is promised for us. But, eternal life does not begin "when the roll is called up yonder." It starts the moment we are restored into God's family.

Heaven, then, is not our ultimate objective in life. But rather it is a gloriously transformed continuation of our lives in God now. The place is relatively unimportant. The personal relationship is that upon which we need to concentrate.

As a child of my parents, I'm not that interested in what I will receive from them in inheritance one day. That will simply be a by-product of kinship. The foundation of our relationship, communication, and closeness is not the expected fortune. Rather it is a strong cord of love that still continues to grow. The value of gifts received now and in the future is intrinsically enclosed within the personal value of our mutual love.

We can apply this to an infinitely greater relationship, that of child to heavenly Father. We need not focus only on our inheritance—that is not what promises to make heaven wonderful. Our love relationship with God is what gives eternity real meaning in our lives. Our lives should be centered in responding to His Father-heart of love. It is here that we find our chief objective in this life, as well as in the life to come.

This One Thing I Do

A few years ago I was tremendously challenged by

20

a response that Dr. Clyde Taylor, associated with the National Association of Evangelicals, made to this interesting question.

"What is your burning desire in life?" an earnest young man inquired.

My ears immediately set their frequency to receive an answer reflecting Dr. Taylor's effective ministry in missions and evangelism. This godly man paused only a moment before he answered quietly, "To obey Jesus, to please Him."

Our ultimate desire, our one objective in life should be this—to bring pleasure to the heart of God. Jesus gave this emphasis when asked to declare the great commandment. "Thou shalt love the Lord thy God with all thy heart, and with all thy soul, and with all thy mind" (Matt. 22:37, *KJV*). The essence of loving God with our whole being—our mind, will and emotions—is that we desire to please Him above all else. I believe this is accomplished in two major ways.

The first way is to joyfully and consistently obey His known commands, and to grow in sensitivity to His Spirit's directives. This is inherent in any good father-child relationship. I know some of my dad's wishes because he verbally related them to me. I know other of his desires because I've spent meaningful time getting to know him. My love in action to him is glad obedience to his authority and a desire to know more of what pleases him. This should be our response to the far greater love of God.

The second avenue in accomplishing our objective is one that Jesus gives in the next verse. "Thou shalt love thy neighbor as thyself" (Matt. 22:39, *KJV*). Applied, this means that by accepting myself, I am free to equally accept others, and demonstrate God's

21

quality of love to them. In realizing my significance to God as an individual I can see others as significant individuals too. I can genuinely love them because God loves them and I love Him and desire to please Him.

If we keep the desire to delight our Father's heart as a single motivating force in our lives, we will have a sense of balance. We will be rightly related to God as well as to our fellowmen. And when time ends, God will complete His transforming work in us. 'We shall be like him; for we shall see him as he is" (1 John 3:2, *KJV*.) Throughout eternity our thankful hearts will continue to worship Him, perfectly loving Him and the fellow citizens of His kingdom. Thus, our chief objective in this life will be one that will continue to motivate us forever.

Our Central Intelligence Agency

Let's lower the eyebrows raised by the ending of chapter 1. Evangelism is certainly part of the response to Jesus' commission to His disciples and must be obeyed. But the privilege of being a channel through which the Holy Spirit works is limited to this life only. In our eternal future "every knee shall bow ... and every tongue shall confess that Jesus Christ is Lord, to the glory of God the Father" (Phil. 2:10, 11, *TLB*).

To be godly men and women in respective ordained roles is essential in God's economy in time and space. Yet, sex differentiation is also limited to the parenthesis of time in the flow of eternity. These are two of many worthwhile goals for which to strive, but unless they blend into our eternal objective, they can lead to frustration and defeat.

Let's think of it as traveling. A trip may have many interesting and exciting moments, but few buy tickets simply for the ride. The purpose of the fare is to reach a desired destination.

The trip, although absolutely essential to reach the destination, is not the objective of the journey. There may be several stops, layovers, schedule changes and perhaps even breakdowns. But the traveler who is focusing on his ultimate destination and is assured by the pilot that it will be reached, can adjust to interruptions and delays. The passenger who is along only for the ride will most likely feel unfulfilled and thwarted.

I may feel inclined to enter a certain sphere of Christian work, a worthwhile goal to set. But if that goal is not seen as the mode of transportation to reach my higher objective, or destination, I will probably feel it a burden. For example, I may feel it is right for me to commit myself to some area of overseas work. I could view it as my supreme sacrifice and go on my way as a moaning missionary, finding my only joy in the fact that I've paid my due. Separate it, or anything else, from a higher desire to please God's heart and the good goal can become a deathly dirge. If circumstances, such as poor health, should prevent me from achieving a specific goal, I am lost and disillusioned.

Don't misunderstand me . . . I believe in missions wholeheartedly. I've been actively investigating the possibility of personal involvement in this area just this year. But I see it not as an end in itself. Rev. Bill Harding, a respected mission leader, once told me, "It's your *relation*, not your location or vocation, that's really important."

I like that!

The individual, living with this philosophy, should

23

be known for his flexibility. He can find opportunity to achieve his objective in any setting with any circumstance. Even seemingly insignificant daily goals, such as accomplishing a certain amount of work in a specific period of time, can fit into the developing portrait of a God-pleasing life. If interruptions or irritations destroy that perfect schedule, he sees them as just a different method by which he can accomplish his objective.

A recent example of this has not even had the opportunity to cool off, it's so fresh from the oven. As I have been writing today, a record number of unrehearsed breaks have occurred. The most recent was embodied in my six-year-old niece, Mary, asking for a promised favor. Should I let my creative spurt sputter out, or should I consider this a special appointment to be kept? Mary and I had a great time together and I have not lost time for a moment in what is really important.

We tend to make Christian living so terribly complex and difficult. We get bogged down by do's and don'ts; condemned by did's and didn'ts; and defeated by done's and can't-be-undone's. If our lives were lived daily in conscious awareness of one objective, to please God, wouldn't we be experiencing God's highest? Our life-style, our decision-making policies, our interpersonal relationships would all be controlled by this "central intelligence agency."

Man vs. Woman vs. Person

We can all share this common objective in life—to please God's heart, but our modes of transportation (goals) are varied. There are as many different "models" as there are individuals. Remember that we are all individuals in God's sight. We may range from roller skates to rockets, but God has designed our vehicles of transport to give each of us the best trip possible.

So our goals, whether daily, monthly or life-long, build up the mileage and are extremely important. If they are severed from the mainline, no matter how worthy they may be, they become basically selfish. We can accomplish all sorts of wonderful things for His kingdom but if our motive is not to please Him then we have been unfaithful.

A couple of inherent factors in addition to our individuality have a great deal of influence as to our motivation on "how we run." The first is the hood we are driving behind—one of two body types, manhood or womanhood. The second is whether we operate solo or duo. But our fulfillment will not be found in either factor of sex or marital status. Both of these specifics should blend together in contributing toward the higher objective without becoming ends in themselves.

A few months ago, one of my students about to become a Mrs. was sharing some of her feelings about being a woman and an almost-married one. She asked me a question that really stimulated my thinking. "Are you more importantly a person or a woman, Virginia?"

I floundered around the first few minutes in some jumbled response and finally concluded, "Sorry, I just can't separate the two. I cannot be a complete person without being a complete woman. Neither can I be a complete woman without being a complete person. And I can be neither a complete person or woman if I am not reaching toward higher ground, 'to be conformed to the image of his Son' (Rom. 8:29). That means to daily be more resembling a perfect Father-pleasing child, as Jesus was."

Sex differentiation is a very special provision of God in creation. When God was writing the script of Genesis I don't believe for one minute that Act II—enter Eve—was an afterthought. God created papa and mama beasts and commanded them to be fruitful and multiply. Adam made the scene solo and for the first time the Creator decreed, "Not good." The situation gave way to the world's most beautiful and exciting love story. But we'll get to this later.

Marriage vs. Unmarriage vs. Fulfillment

Perhaps the most sensitive factor in our "vehicle" is whether we are operating with a copilot or are still "unclaimed freight," as my married sister teasingly labels me. Our subtle nature, with a little help from the master liar, proclaims this the central point around which our energies should revolve. The unwed see their potential stunted without a life partner. The married often feel they have no opportunity to "find themselves," to be truly liberated.

I've gained insight from my sister along these lines. She has always been interested and involved in music, in which she is very talented. Since her family happened, further formal study has been delayed and daily practice sessions are often impossible. She could feel unfulfilled, halted in her prime and fret over her undeveloped genius. Yet, she strives to joyfully accept her role as wife and mother, and to see it as her priority for this time.

Her role gives her all kinds of opportunities to be creative in the song of selflessness, music that truly delights God. She sees her goal of developing her musical talent only temporarily delayed and when it becomes feasible to pursue it, she will. This goal will also have a higher purpose and greater enjoyment and appreciation because she has waited.

What a preparation for LIFE—not just marriage—to practice living and demonstrating selfless love. Much has been said and written on the various roles in life—of the man, the woman, the married, the unmarried, and combinations within. There are good thoughts within this context but sometimes these supposed roles can confine and stereotype.

I am not playing the role of a "single woman." I am playing my own part—especially written by my Director. The central theme of that part is the acting out of a selfless quality of love daily. If I "I do" someday, my priorities and responsibilities will certainly change but the basic me will not.

Different experiences give different perspectives, but the development of the "inside you" goes on as a continuous process. Age and experience don't necessarily change us; they may only deepen old patterns.

God is in the business of transforming. "We can be mirrors that brightly reflect the glory of the Lord. And as the Spirit of the Lord works within us, we become more and more like him" (2 Cor. 3:18, *TLB*).

We begin first by seeing ourselves as a special person by redemption and creation. Our new relationship with God gives a unifying thrust for living—to please God by returning His selfless love with our mind, will, and emotions. We see contentment in our sex and marital status related to that main objective. But let's get back to that garden love story . . . .

THREE
FOR MEN AND WOMEN ONLY

Wouldn't it be exciting if we could see instant replays of biblical history? I'm voting for that during the millennium. I'd love to see the expression on Adam's face when he awakened, one rib short, to find lovely Eve by his side.

After the initial "Wow!" he probably gave her some line like, 'Haven't we met around the garden somewhere?"

Eve, silently swallowing her "Whoopee!" probably responded, "Well no, you see I'm new in town, but I've got a feeling in my bones that we've met somewhere too."

Don't let my levity distract from the wonder of that moment. Adam, after naming and observing all the animals, was surely aware of complementary pairs. He had spent time alone and now was experiencing the completion of God's perfect work. Think of his thrill when he saw Eve and took her into his arms, knowing that she was a part of him.

Mankind had reached completion as a specially created unit. Adam responded with, "This is now bone of my bones, and flesh of my flesh; she shall be called Woman, because she was taken out of Man" (Gen. 2:23, *KJV*).

Then a direct quote from the Creator is given. "Therefore shall a man leave his father and his mother, and shall cleave unto his wife; and they shall be one flesh" (Gen. 2:24, *KJV*).

Jesus confirms this to be God's statement, then adds, in Matthew 19:6, "What therefore God hath joined together, let not man put asunder." This gives us a full picture of the permanence that God intends for the marriage relationship.

From Created Perfection to Chaos

It is significant that Eve was fashioned from the flesh of Adam and not from the dust of the earth as Adam had been. The quote from St. Augustine is familiar. "If God meant woman to rule over man, He would have taken her out of Adam's head. Had He designed her to be his slave, He would have taken her from his feet, but God took woman out of man's side, for He made her to be a helpmeet, an equal to him."

To me the most exciting fact of the whole creation story is that men and women are quite literally part of one another, they are made from "one flesh." They were created to be a team for accomplishing God's purposes as well as for their own enjoyment. This makes the "battle of the sexes" pretty ridiculous and tragically sad.

"We've come a long way, baby," but I'm afraid it's in the wrong direction.

That beautiful garden was also the setting for the beginning of that downhill tread when man and woman chose their own selfish way. Francis Schaeffer calls the result of the Fall the "beginning of great separations"—separation of God from man, man from himself, man from man, and man from nature.

"Adam was separated from Eve. Both of them immediately tried to pass off blame for the Fall. This signals the loss of the possibility of their walking truly side by side in Utopian democracy.

" 'And thy desire shall be to thy husband, and he shall rule over thee.' In a fallen world, pure democracy is not possible. Rather, God brings structure into the primary relationship of man— the man-woman relationship.

"In a fallen world (in every kind of society, big and small and in every relationship) structure is needed for order. God Himself here imposes it on the basic human relationship. Form is given and without such form freedom would only be chaos."[1]

Chaos is an appropriate term to describe the present relationship between men and women. By rejecting God's principle of male leadership we reject the formula for healthy, free relationships. God longs to restore the complementary unity that He created but, apart from His ordained order, it is impossible.

Bridge of Love and Respect

The concept of submission has been misunderstood and misapplied until its original intent is almost lost. No creature escapes submission to a higher authority. Instead of viewing submission as a top to bottom hierarchy, we need to see this loving, protective order of God as a side by side relationship. In the man-woman relationship, instead of looking down at the one who is to be obedient, let's look across at the one to whom God has given a particular responsibility.

30

Paul writes of this order to the Corinthian church, known for their chaotic disorder:

"But there is one matter I want to remind you about: that a wife is responsible to her husband, her husband responsible to Christ, and Christ is responsible to God" (1 Cor. 11:3, *TLB*).

Paul gives additional relationships of responsibility in Ephesians:

"Children, obey your parents; this is the right thing to do because God has placed them in authority over you . . . . Slaves (or employees), obey your masters (or employers); be eager to give them your very best. Serve them as you would Christ" (Eph. 6:1,5, *TLB*).

These relationships do not threaten or insult our freedom and dignity—they define it! And in it all, we can see that God designed a certain response to one another that, if exercised, restores the original oneness of creation.

Having established that point, let's get back to the man-woman relationship. Here again Paul writes:

"You wives must submit to your husband's leadership in the same way you submit to the Lord . . . . And you husbands, show the same kind of love to your wives as Christ showed to the church when he died for her" (Eph. 5:22,25, *TLB*).

This is a beautiful God-intended relationship that should be enjoyed, not ignored within the marital union. The man is to love, the woman is to respect, and the exchange soon weaves a bridge of love and respect from both directions.

My brother married a few years ago and the wedding celebration included these vows which I believe reflect a beautiful exchange of love and respect, the biblical plan for the ultimate unity and happiness:

"Karen, I love you,
   and in total commitment give you my life.
"My love for you is all pervasive,
   but especially deep in that oneness we enjoy
   through union with God's Son.
   It is my fulfillment to love and cherish you,
   even as myself.
"It is my delight to hold you
   in the very highest esteem.
   Your love for me, Karen, is indeed treasured
   above all earthly values.
"I ask you to accept my love."

"I love you, Stephen,
   and with joy commit my life to you.
   You have added a new dimension to my life
   by loving me as I am.
"Your love is patient, kind, and understanding.
   I respond to that love, and desire to love you
   more perfectly as we share life together.
"I desire to be your complement
   in every area of life—
   to experience your joys and sorrows,
   to care for you, and meet your needs.
"I promise to follow your loving leadership
   and honor and respect your judgments
   as we walk together as one in God's ways."

Poor Paul is often accused of arrogant, chauvinis-
tic views. Much of what he teaches regarding women,
however, relates to cultural norms or problems within
a specific church. There is much to indicate that he

highly respected and admired women as equal in God's sight. He often mentions them by name in his letters.

Paul makes a decisive, equalitarian statement in the following:

"But remember that in God's plan men and women need each other. For although the first woman came out of man, all men have been born from women ever since, and both men and women come from God their Creator" (1 Cor. 11:11,12, *TLB*).

God designed man and woman to be a unit with certain division of labor. Man's role is to love, provide and protect. Woman's role is to respect man's leadership to be "mother of all living," the generic meaning of Eve.

Singles Too!

What does all this say to those men and women who are unmarried? Are they excluded from this norm of companionship and principle of God's order? Not at all. The original concept of mutual respect and esteem, and a blending together in companionship is definitely not for marrieds only. But more about that later.

One principle that governs all of God's created— both men and women—is the responsibility of the one in authority to lead, and of the protected one to respect that leadership. I believe that the natural order, in men-women relationships, is that the man is the initiator and the woman is the responder. However, a woman should not feel compelled to *obey* any man, except her husband. Yet she can respect and encourage the man who takes the leadership role in a relationship. And this concept does not lessen my personal integrity nor my individuality, but enhances both!

The "quiet and meek spirit" is not a feminine personality type, but rather it is an inward beauty of a soul. This spirit does not claim its own rights but joyfully accepts authority, whether it be God, the government, father, husband or employer. This, you see, does not eliminate anyone from needing a meekness of heart.

Tinkerbell vs. Tarzan

The traditional and current concepts of masculinity and femininity contend that there are vast psychological differences between men and women. Men have been considered the initiators and women the responders.

A man is depicted as logical, rational, active and aggressive. A woman is emotional, dependent, passive and warmly responsive. A man is seen as objective, direct and democratic. A woman is subjective, sensitive and given to intuitive partiality.

Maybe . . . just maybe.

I can't personally affirm this either/or mentality. There may be tendencies; whether they are a result of a genetic gift or cultural patterns, I'm not qualified to discern.

Let's attempt to approach realistically what masculinity and femininity should truly involve. Contrary to the age-weathered concept, it is not the bold, conquering possessiveness of the male animal versus the frailty, coyness or pushing helplessness of the female. Since my frame of reference is genetically female, I'll define first what I believe femininity should be.

A woman who is feminine is one who genuinely likes herself and is comfortable and "at home" within her body and personality.

She is excited about being a lady, joyfully and graciously accepting God's gift of genes. One writer describes such a woman!

"The unforgettable woman has a deep core of 'aloneness.' She is a person in her own right. She has a sense of serenity and personal security, that some of her joys are inward, that she has a satisfying existence in her own mind and imagination. This integrity and inward richness keeps such a woman from any slavish desire to please. It gives her a wonderful simplicity and protects her from fussiness and pettiness . . . ."[2]

A feminine woman also genuinely likes and appreciates men because she earnestly respects them, not because of the praise, admiration or value they give her.

She does not cower to them as her superiors or disdainfully snub them as her inferiors.

She recognizes their responsibility of leadership with appreciation, not resentment.

She refuses to play ego-building games for selfish advantage, but strives to accomplish the position of complement.

She helps men enjoy their responsibility of manhood.

She demonstrates her admiration and appreciation without being immodest or threatening.

She is not preoccupied with "rings and strings," but rather has a genuine desire to know and like men as individuals, as "singles."

Such a woman gives evidence of a growing sensitivity—that intuitive ability to recognize and meet others' needs.

She is perfectly free to give herself, having a deep capacity to love.

She knows how to listen intently as if the person who is speaking to her and what he is saying are most important: and she means it. She has the intelligence, wisdom and experience to make such listening a joy for herself and others.

She knows when to speak and when to remain silent.

She knows when to empathetically comfort and when to supportively challenge.

Consistently and lovingly, she is sensitive to know if her presence is needed or if her absence is better.

She does not recycle everyone's problems through her own life's experiences, insisting that she understands all; but she gently identifies with the person when possible and then directs the hurt to the One who does understand all.

A feminine woman is also responsive—a natural outgrowth of sensitivity.

She demonstrates a "joy of the moment" zest for living.

She is drawn to beauty, especially the everyday pleasures such as sunsets, honeysuckle and bluebirds.

She can transform awkward, embarrassing moments to funny, unforgettable times.

She has the talent of putting people at ease and accepted—all types of people in all types of situations regardless of who they are or what the situation is.

She exposes hidden assets and talents in others which only need encouragement to appear.

She has an unquenchable thirst for learning, for experiencing new adventures. She enthusiastically pursues the development of her special God-given potential in all areas of her life.

That, to me, is what a feminine woman is.

If I were to define the masculine male, I would use exacly the preceding virtues, with one exception; concerning leadership: "He recognizes his responsibility of leadership with a humble desire for wisdom, not a gloating pride of position!"

So, you see, in the opinion of at least one person— a feminine woman and "real man" have equal and similar characteristics. True masculinity and femininity are not to be found in the Tinkerbell versus Tarzan syndrome. It goes much deeper than just body types, clothes and manner of expression.

True masculinity and femininity are rooted in the development of strong character and selfless love. A dominating, aggressive woman is unattractive, not because she is "unfeminine," but because she displays basic selfishness. A timid, fearful man is unattractive, not because he is "unmasculine," but because he reveals a lack of self-acceptance and purpose.

The genuinely masculine man and feminine woman are living meaningfully because they accept themselves and the gender God gave them. They focus on one objective—to live a life that is pleasing to God. In order to accomplish this in the natural, everyday events of life they must commit themselves to reflect the revealed character of God. This is a continuous process of choosing the best and eliminating anything less.

Although they are consciously aware of their objective, their spontaneity is not squelched by a "does it please God for me to breathe now?" hangup. Their central thrust to please God becomes a natural part of their daily decisions, and they live with growing freedom to be all that God intended. They are in the business of "you're not getting older, you're getting better." They desire to build this strength of character and integrity by disciplined, expectant living.

Yes Different, But ...

I'm certainly not suggesting that there are, or should be, no differences between male and female. Structural and functional diversities cannot be denied, and who in the world wants to!? It would be a dull, drab world without the differences in looks, dress, gestures and manner of expression between persons of similar gender—but much more so between male and female.

Clothes reflect much of how a person sees himself. It is sad to see a person dress in a way that proclaims to the world that his measure of self-worth is determined by the way the opposite sex sees him. Costume may also broadcast an insecurity of sexual identity if he attempts to mimic the opposite sex.

Voice tone, walk and gestures should also be in keeping with the biological and cultural norms. A squeaky, rubber-wristed man or a bellowing, back-slapping woman is just not attractive.

Whether biological or cultural, certain tendencies are evident and demonstrated regularly. The strong emotional nature of a woman absorbs her in motherhood and in mothering-type involvements, which is God's plan.

But men have demonstrated equal emotional depth, although it may be expressed differently.

Remember it is the man who has the responsibility to love in the order of God's unity. Most women readily agree that one of the most attractive traits in a man is tenderness, the evidence of "controlled strength."

The rational, objective nature of a man equips him to provide and protect, which is God's natural order. Yet women can exercise excellent logic, even when it is camouflaged with emotional tones. These women of wisdom are respected and admired and depended upon by men, as well as other women.

Individuals of both sexes need to genuinely like themselves and members of the opposite sex, appreciating the divine plan of unity. They need to develop sensitivity and responsiveness as they learn more of God's quality of selfless love. They will then be free to express themselves as men and women in their own right.

Such individuals can happily maintain within cultural norms without feeling stereotyped. They have a deep sense of personal and sexual identity. They will cease fire in the battle of the sexes and enter not a regime of peaceful coexistence, but a reign of perfect complementation. This is part of God's highest for us .... It is the standard which pleases Him.

And what a way to live!

Now, there may be remaining feelings of "Sounds terrific, but I'm just not in that groove. How can I have that God-ordained relationship without marriage? How can I provide and protect without a family? How can I respond and 'mother' without a home?

"Isn't marriage, after all, the determinant of fulfillment?"

Footnotes

1. Excerpted from *Genesis in Space and Time* by Francis A. Schaeffer. ©
1972 by L'Abri Fellowship, Switzerland, pages 97, 98, 103. Used by permission of InterVarsity Press, USA.
2. Ardis Whitman, "The Unforgettable Woman" from *The Marriage Affair*,
ed. J. Allan Peterson, (Wheaton, Illinois: Tyndale House Publishers, 1971),
p. 116.

FOUR
IF MARRIAGE IS THE ANSWER, WHAT'S THE QUESTION?

"To be or not to be"—married, that is—is just *not* the question!

Each week one or two remarks come my way such as, "Isn't it about time for you to find some nice young man?" (I didn't know they were hiding) or "Why in the world are you still unmarried?"

A close friend, a lively middle-aged young maid, is often asked the indelicate question of "What happened?" She invariably replies, with serious demeanor, "I just haven't found a man that deserves to be as happy as I could make him," ending with a mischievous grin. At times she postscripts, "And it's taken so long to acquire this state of blissfulness, I can't easily relinquish it." Her busy effective life with many happy involvements has no time for wistfulness. She's still "ready any time for the right man" but manages a rich, full life in the now.

But the impression of the majority is still that marriage is the key to life's fulfillment, and those without it should be pitied or at least suspected. A sharp observer of life once asked, "If marriage is the answer, what's the question?"

Left Out or Trapped In?

What *is* the place of this blessed institution in God's economy? How should individuals within and without view its significance?

The twentieth century culture still finds marriage a norm, even though the legal family-unit concept is rapidly declining in popularity. The Christian community, reacting to this threat on marital solidity, defends its sanctity and sociological value, and justly so. The unmarried populace is often caught in the crossfire of the two camps.

The world may accuse the unwed of stodgy, naive life-styles, pity them for their lack of sexual involvement and explain one situation with the other. You know the saying, "Good girls always finish last."

The church, while outwardly commending their "sacrifice," may inwardly suspect their character and true nature. Any exposed weakness or fault is transcribed into "Well, I can certainly understand why he (she) isn't married!" Few activities are planned in the church life for these unmarrieds past college age, who perhaps need this type of fellowship and encouragement the most.

Some of the so-called "victims" of this unmarried fate are frustrated and confused, not only by this external prejudice but also by internal pressures. "What's wrong with me?" can become a deadly game that is only a code-phrase for "What's wrong with God?"

When friends and relatives have all walked the aisle, and you're left holding the bag—of rice, it's perhaps a natural reaction to wonder, "Why not me?" But natural isn't healthy if encouraged by further poor me's and lucky them's. This malignancy of resentment and bitterness may destroy any potential for fulfillment even if the future does bring the heavenly honeymoon and happy hearth.

On the other hand, marrieds also are victims of similar kinds of doubts and discouragements. Many have entered into society's norm and now wish, perhaps secretly, that they could exit through another of this world's norms—divorce. They may be disillusioned with the mundane routines, the unromantic chores and even lonely isolation. Expecting the partner to know and accept all, they soon retreat from true communication when criticized or misunderstood.

They read about the open marriage concept, verbally "Tsh, tsh" but secretly wonder if it's not such a bad idea. They read about the joys of a Christian marriage, verbally "Amen!" but secretly wonder how in the world to do it. Confined by their work or household chores from doing "what I've always wanted to do," they contract that same germ of "Why not me?" from which bitterness and resentment grow.

I don't mean to infer that no one in this world is truly happy and satisfied. I have met scores of individuals with and without the marital experience who are very content. But there is a harvest of examples of unfulfilled, unhappy life-styles and the crop isn't pure-bred. Both sides of the matrimonial fence have their share in this category.

43

So, "To be or not to be . . . . "

Is complete personal fulfillment really possible inside marriage where commitment to mate and children consume all time and energy? Is complete personal fulfillment really possible outside of marriage—the planned milieu to complete the creation-intended unity of persons?

The answer to both of these questions is a resounding "Yes!" It seems impossible for some people to be completely fulfilled apart from marriage. It also seems impossible for others to be completely fulfilled apart from nonmarriage.

Each one of us was intricately designed and sovereignly placed in an environment. God knows each person's fulfillment formula and will provide it, if we trust Him to do so. The correct vehicle of transport—marriage or non-marriage—is dependent on the unique traveler. God knows us infinitely better than we know ourselves, and He knows if we will reach our objective better solo or duo. And here again is where we go below the surface to see the heart of the matter.

Because of how our machinery operates, what pleases God is identical to what fulfills us. We do not worship a selfish God who seeks only glory, but a wise Father who desires only the best for His beloved children.

My brother-in-law placed this quote under his wife's picture before they were married: "God gives only His best to those who leave the choice up to Him." To find the deepest, richest, fullest quality of living is to be consistently living with one thrust. So in essence, what pleases God is exactly the intent of His great selfless love toward us.

If we view marital status as an end in itself, we are

destined to be defeated and disappointed—whether we are married or not. If we view marital status as a condition to be enjoyed and utilized in meeting a higher objecti ., we are destined for fulfillment—whether married or not. This is our major premise. And in this foundational context, we now consider some specifics.

Marriage: Mission Possible

Marriage is not only a norm in modern thinking, it is God's norm. As we have seen, He gives it special treatment in His story of beginnings. He designed the necessity of two to be fruitful and multiply, but not only biologically. Within the marriage covenant, personal and spiritual growth also are to be multiplied and nurtured.

Marriage is a channel through which God has accomplished many of His purposes in the world. The story of Esther who, through her royal marriage, rescued the Jewish people, would have made world headlines in her time. Her intervention was extremely significant in history and directly in our lives. Remember, Jesus came through the Jewish line.

God provides ultimate unity and satisfaction for most through the marriage norm. The beautiful love stories of Isaac and Rebekah, and Boaz and Ruth illustrate His desire to provide the right person at the right time for the right reasons.

God uses the marriage union as a concrete example of His desired oneness with believers. The church is often referred to as the "bride of Christ." This should not only give us extremely high standards for which to strive im Christian marriage, but also the clue that God ordained it for the vast majority. The

45

deep oneness of body, soul, and spirit that is pervasive in the mutual commitment of marriage cannot be duplicated in any other earthly relationship.

All of these give those who are presently in the state of unmatrimony a logical and sufficient reason to expect an overthrow of their state someday. That includes me, by the way, and I'm enjoying that expectancy.

A younger gal once asked me with a troubled frown, "Virginia, are you resigned never to be married?"

"Certainly not!" I laughingly replied, "I've only just begun." Such resignation to the so-called plague of petunias and pussycats isn't for me. If I never join the ranks of God's norm, it won't be out of resignation. I firmly believe that if I reach God's presence without the marital experience, it will be with joyful confirmation—not resignation—that He has provided His best for me; nothing less.

Some teach that one should discover whether his gift in life is the married or unmarried role, and go to it. Sounds O.K., but I'm not sure just how to determine such a gift. It is true that some unmarrieds are involved in ministries or professions which would make a good family life difficult or impossible. But life is not static, and although married life may be unwise now, who is to say what the future has in store. Only a closed attitude of "This is my thing, and I'll do it 'til I die" excludes marriage. Others may claim to prefer the uncomplicated life of no mate, no babies.

It seems to be realistically healthy to see marriage as God's norm, and to see yourself as part, or part-to-be, of His created plan for unity and companionship. This doesn't conclude that those who never utter, "I will" are the "leftovers" in God's world. In a unique way, they may be the "let-ins" to a very special category of His exceptions.

Certainly, God knows when a particular individual's fulfillment formula equals an unmarried life, and to it He brings an abundant capacity for rich living. An individual who graciously accepts this formula with thanksgiving can experience an exciting, challenging life. This does not eliminate expectancy—fulfillment through unmarried living may only be Phase I in God's program. Those who are life-long exceptions to God's norm, if they are rightly related to God and His purposes for them, will not finish life with unmet expectations, but superceded ones.

Having a unique viewpoint of the love and all-sufficiency of God, the unmarried can enjoy a fellowship with God that is special—not better but perhaps different. Interpersonal relationships may be more extensive and deep. The unmarried can be creative in revolving his life around many others to escape self-centeredness. With a little effort, he can experience meaningful relationships of protecting, providing or fostering.

He does not depend on another to dictate his personal value or worth. His interests and experiences may be broader, especially in terms of job mobility and travel. He has a very special impact on others as he demonstrates unselfish love in living color with a firm conviction of the faithful goodness of God.

Again, the unmarried life is God's *exception*, with few chosen participants. Others may volunteer or by apathetic resignation be drafted into the ranks, for it's sad but true that many who are living unhappily outside of God's norm need not be there. Without a healthy expectancy or acceptance of self and sexuality, they have become unattractively ingrown, with an undercurrent of bitterness.

An active campaign to regain a proper perspective of life as God intended it to be may change not only attitudes and an unsatisfying life. It may create an attractive winsomeness that just might be the channel through which God's norm is reached. Now, if we should expect marriage as God's norm, what does, or does not, that expectancy mean?

Trinket or Pure Gold?

To expect marriage does not mean that we narrow our focus to the details—what, how, where, when, and who. The "what" we will get from marriage cannot be exactly predicted with our limited foresight. Only hindsight enjoys that privilege.

Yet an honest exploration of what is involved in a godly marriage is certainly worthwhile and exposure to good written material and realistic living situations is helpful. But if we build pre- and post-wedding fantasies on current romantic propaganda, we're not being fair to ourselves. Living up to those unrealistic expectations is impossible and disappointment may be deep.

The details of "where" we find our marriage partners can't be part of our planning either. It is interesting that Rebekah was minding her own business in Genesis 24, being naturally gracious and kind, when her proposal came. The sound principle of enjoying a useful life—developing qualities of generosity and sensitivity—is found in this story.

A pastor friend of mine teasingly asks when he sees me if I've found any new wells lately, or if I've been watering camels in my spare time. There's no crime in going where the action is—the community well was also the social gathering place of that day. But to join groups and clubs, go to Christian colleges or prompt friends to "fix you up" with the sole purpose of helping God out a little, isn't exactly how we would describe waiting with joyful expectancy.

The desire to socialize with members of the opposite sex is great and the norm of companionship should be enjoyed freely. But the desperate schemer is never an attractive person. By the way, that category isn't reserved to the classic prowling female. The men may have more subtle tactics, but they have their share in this "I'd rather do it myself" approach.

Neither should we sit around, waiting for the blessed event to converge and knock heads together. This is no more expectancy than "senior panic." People who practice datelessness to prove their amazing ability to let God provide, may only be displaying an inability to develop wholesome person-centered relationships. Remember that accomplishment isn't avoiding through abstinence, but controlling by experience. So join groups, go to college, even splurge on a sensible blind date now and then. But get your motives and fears untangled.

Healthy expectancy does not measure "when." It does not look to the months and years ahead and set a target date for marriage. Neither does it narrow itself to "who."

Quite a few years ago, a fellow asked me if I honestly believed that there was only one man in the world for me. My reply was something like this, "Well, if there is only one or a million for me, my standards for discerning who I will marry are the same. And I'd just as soon believe him to be one in a million, the only one in the whole world for me.

"It seems that if God has made me such a unique creature, He has also made another one that I complement, who is equipped to complete me. We will complete the intended unity not only because I'm female and he's male, but because I'm me and he's he."

When I was five, my parents took me to a toy store on my birthday and told me to pick out my present, within certain limitations, of course. I must have scrutinized every article five times before I made the great decision. Do you know what I chose? A creepy, rubber spider that menacingly flexed his eight biceps when squeezed! Ugh! Today the one critter I despise is a spider, large or small. But mysteriously at the age of five, its likeness was the desire of my heart.

I had a birthday just recently and this time my parents gave me a lovely golden ring. God promises that if we delight ourselves in Him, He will give us the desires of our heart (Psalm 37:4). I'm no Hebrew scholar, but I think the real meaning of that verse is this: As we base our fulfillment and satisfaction on God, He will continue to purify and bring to maturity the desires of our heart. Then He gladly provides them. Who wants to stop with a rubber spider when a golden ring and more are in store?

Hands Open to God

Discernment and appreciation expand with time and experience. Our Father knows the right moment and the right mate to meet and supercede all of our expectations. Assured that God is sovereign in our lives when we strive to please Him, our choice of "who" is reached through the avenue of good, sanctified common sense that is practically oriented.

Personal and spiritual growth should occur with time; therefore, our compatibility quotient should also increase. A maturing understanding of self and others also gives a more realistic definition of compatibility.

Martin Luther, one of God's special exceptions, pictured expectancy as simply holding open hands to God. We are free to enjoy things and people who come into our hands, yet we should not grasp and hold on and call them "mine." How it hurts when our fingers must be pried loose. We should continue to keep our hands open to Him and be fully confident in His wisdom of giving and taking.

My dad used to lovingly tell me, his spoiled youngest, "Baby, I'd give you anything in the world if it was good for you." When I made a request, I would expect one of two answers from him. It was either, "No, honey, I love you and that's not best for you now," or "Yes, I love you and believe that it is good for you now." This is a very homemade example, but so illustrative of an infinitely greater wisdom and love.

I remember one specific occasion during my college days, when the memory of my dad's love quieted my anxiousness. Mr. Tall-Dark-and-Handsome entered my acquaintance, and I really wanted to date him. The day arrived when I knew it was now or never. But my hopes plunged as he left the library without so much as a hello my way.

At that moment I remembered Dad's promise and could almost hear my heavenly Father say, "Honey, I'd give you anything in the world if it was good for you." It was so close, so precious to my childish heart. It quieted my fears and disappointment.

Just Too Far Away?

A further word to those who, such as I, are still in the stage of expectancy. Lest, I seem to gloss over some of the real day-to-day problems of our status with a sweet coating of spiritual pieties, let me share several of my "downers" with you. Most of my peers are married, and it's easy to feel that I'm on the periphery of that inner circle. As close as I may be to some of them, it is impossible to completely share their problems or joys.

Although I do enjoy close friends, there is no one with whom I can share the minor details, those irritating or exciting moments of every day. At times in the stillness of the night I long for that someone with whom to share those intimate secrets. I also project to the future and wonder what old age will hold if I have no children, no family to care for me.

I once thought it was quite spiritual to desire nothing more than the life I was presently given to enjoy. How victorious I felt when loneliness and longing weren't nagging at my heart; sometimes that high would actually last for weeks! How sad and defeated I felt when marriage and family seemed just too far away.

One of those defeated days ended and I despondently tossed a bride's magazine down with, "Oh, what's the use!" The guilt poured in and threatened to keep me awake most of the night. I confessed and re-confessed, but still felt restless and unsettled.

Knowing I had a full day's work ahead the next day, I finally dragged myself out of bed to try and find some sort of pill to put me to sleep. In my mind God seemed to say, "Virginia, dear, get back in bed. I'm trying to tell you something and I don't want some pill to interfere." Only moments later He quieted my fears and guilt and gave restful sleep.

His loving revelation at that time was this, "I created you in a certain way and put you in a close, loving family for a specific reason. To be defeated and feel guilty because you desire a husband and home are to deny what I created and am nurturing in you.

"I understand your loneliness ... after all, I was unmarried as I lived on earth. It's not wrong for you to want marriage, it's My norm and the way I made you!" Since that night I've recognized that impatience and self-pity are wrong, but the basic desire to complete God's creation plan is good and right.

My expectations are based on God, His goodness, and the way He has made me. Recently, when I was struggling with a decision, my college pastor told me, "You don't have to find God's will, you *are* God's will!"

That's an overwhelming command and promise!

To waste a single day with a resigned, apathetic sense of waiting is not expectancy. Our command throughout Scripture to "wait on Jehovah" challenges us to rest confidently in His sufficiency, not to half-way patiently look for a better lot in life.

Get with it now! Don't spend time and energy preparing for life ... live now, enthusiastically, creatively and with expectancy. Expect, and thank God for His very best in your life now and in the years to come.

FIVE
PHYSICAL DEVELOPMENT: BODY BEAUTIFUL

Stop a few moments and walk over to the nearest mirror—full-length preferably. Take a good, long look—head to toe—eye to eye. Before you become too entranced, bored or disgusted, come back and let's talk about that reflection.

What did you see? Was it the real you? Futhermore, did you like that collection of skin and bones staring back at you? Ever wish it could be sent back for remodeling?

Working in the field of medicine, I suppose it could be said that I'm in the body business. The human body is a magnificent structural and functional corporation of delicate, precise instruments. Not only is the "ham bone connected to the knee bone," but the heart and lungs have quite an affair going too. Right down to the cellular level, there's an exciting interdependent working order.

Don't panic—I'm not about to deliver a lecture on DNA and related mysteries. I'm just emphasizing that we've inherited a pretty special people package. If you'd like to do some fascinating exploring, try taking a trip inside your own body via a text of simple anatomy or physiology. It's quite an adventure!

No Split Personality

Some may be thinking at this point, "Let's get it over with, tell us to take our vitamins, jog, or try a new hairstyle. Let's go on to more essential material. Aren't other areas of development *really* more important than the physical?"

I'll give a dogmatic "No," but also qualify that answer with further explanation. Physical, sexual, emotional, social, mental and spiritual development cannot be isolated from one another or listed by priority. Our emphasis is not the distinction between each area, but the healthy integration of the total person. Our purpose is to become aware of individual potential and become motivated to reach toward God's highest in each area.

Physical well-being is absolutely necessary for full mental and spiritual health. Mental health is impossible without good social interaction. Spiritual development is pervasive in all areas. Our lives shouldn't be dissected into compartments in which we dutifully categorize our activities.

A simple illustration of our tendency to do this is the youth group socials I remember as a teen. Planning sessions always included someone postscripting, "Oh, yes, we'd better have some sort of devotional at the end . . . who volunteers?" In our minds there were two distinct parts of a party—first and foremost ... *fun*! The second part, sadly duty-bound with big, black letters was ... *the spiritual*. I'm all for meaningful social events that include enthusiastic sharing of God's truths. But I don't see this severe dichotomy of life into separate categories of importance as being Jesus' teaching.

It's exciting that Jesus chose a wedding as a setting for His first miracle. Quite naturally and without interruption or delay of festivities, He provided superb wine for the wedding guests. He didn't stop to explain or evoke some great moral principle from His act. He continued to join the celebration with the happy, grateful family.

Was the miracle "spiritual"? of course, as were all of Jesus' works. Did the miracle provide physical refreshment and prevent social embarrassment? Yes, again, and it was one act.

Now, in our consideration of our physical well-being let's keep all this in mind. We're hooked up to be a complex, interrelating heap of protoplasm. God created it all—literally breathed His life into that heap, and it's all important to Him. Jesus' development as a young man is recorded as advanced in "wisdom (mentally) and stature (physically), and in favor with God (spiritually) and men (socially)" (Luke 2:52). He approached people's needs at all levels and gave health to all areas.

Dignified Dust

Let's get back to our mirror experiment—to the body you saw—*your* body. Look down at it now. That hand that's holding the book ... is it just twenty-seven bones with thousands of neurons cooperating with the brain to grasp an object? NO, it's a part of you, a hard part to live without!

We could get deeply—and senselessly—philosophical about the division of the body, soul and spirit. I believe that the immortal part of me is not merely occupying a hollow human frame. My body has been so created to consolidate my total being, to be receptive to God's Spirit.

The location of my soul isn't to be diagrammed, although the still unanswered mysteries of the mind may hint of an immortal resident. The psychiatrist who attempts to rid the troubled mind of guilt is often unsuccessful in smothering moral conscience. Psychologists admit that there is something inexplicable in the mind and personality of a person, but refuse to identify it as "soul."

Whatever we conclude about the union of body and soul, we can be certain that they were never created to be separated. One of the results of the Fall is physical death. Francis Schaeffer defines death as "the dissolution of the total man—unity of the body and soul torn asunder."[1] This gives some explanation of the intense pain, both physical and emotional, that comes with death.

Not only was the body part of perfect creation, it is to be restored to perfection in our promised future. This is the significance of the bodily resurrection of Jesus. Easter gives promise of the coming redemption of our bodies.

Jesus could have returned as a spirit, yet He conquered the curse of sin—the separation of body and soul. His resurrection was actually reunion of His spirit with His earthly body, the body we shall see one day.

"Christ did actually rise from the dead, and has become the first of millions who will come back to life again some day" (1 Cor. 15:20, *TLB*). Paul goes on in this passage to tell us, "For our earthly bodies, the ones we have now that can die, must be transformed into heavenly bodies that cannot perish but will live forever" (v. 53).

Paul uses the analogy of a seed being put into the ground to die in order to bring forth new life. The new plant is different from the seed and each seed will produce a different plant. Our resurrection bodies will be different from the "seed," our present bodies. But those new bodies will also be different from one another.

There's substantial evidence that we will recognize one another in our new upholstery. I don't know about you, but that's exciting to me! It gives me a future in which to look forward to an eternal "face-lift," a supernatural "body-lift." It also tells me that my present body, the "seed"—that reflection in the mirror—is important.

Our present "dignified dust" is important for another reason. If we are redeemed by Christ, our bodies literally house the Holy Spirit. Paul calls us "temples."

The Old Testament tediously details the construction of the Tabernacle in a great amount of space, begats and begots, and other seeming nonessentials. I wonder if some of the ancient scribes yawned over parts of Exodus 25—28 at the intricate, detailed instructions of the construction. Yet God inspired the whole thing and these details give us a graphic picture of the beauty of God's house.

Solomon's Temple is outlined in architectural detail in 1 Kings 6. Both the Tabernacle and the Temple were beautiful, richly adorned, clean, well-cared for, well-proportioned structures. Their beauty reflected the glory of the presence of God Himself.

Since our bodies are temples of the Holy Spirit this analogy should certainly give us an exciting motivation for a body beautification campaign. An attempt to be as attractive as possible need not be due to vanity or self-centeredness, nor even for the normal desire to be eye-pleasing to the opposite sex. Our bodies should be as beautiful, well-cared for, and pleasingly proportioned as the Old Testament Tabernacle and Temple, because we are the present temples of God. We may need to do some remodeling.

Nothing destroys the joy of worship more than a poorly kept, dirty, drab church building. Isn't the lack of personal grooming and hygiene just as disturbing? Extreme cases of such lack are not common in our sophisticated, super-Mr. Clean society. But carelessness in this area is possible, especially when there's no member of the opposite sex to attract.

During my college career, I transferred from a coed school to a predominately female campus—from "America the Beautiful" to "Who Cares, USA." However, as Friday night brought an increase in the male census, there was an accompanying metamorphosis of "Who Cares" to "Glamour City."

Making a special effort to look every inch the best for a special night out is part of the fun of living. But it's also fun to respect your appearance on a consistent, daily basis. And who knows who may be watching!

I remember a startling conversation a number of years ago when one of my professors asked me to stay after class. Wondering what I had flunked, I was unprepared for his comment. "Miss Apple, I just wanted to express my appreciation for the way you come to my class. Your dress and neatness tell me something of your fine character."

I was very grateful for that positive impression. But it also made me regretfully mindful of the many times I had rushed to an early morning class, sleepily ungroomed and usually late. I'm afraid that my "fine character" was a bit unnoticed on those occasions.

Hey, Good-Looking

God must certainly enjoy a handsome, healthy temple. And doesn't it feel great to know that you are looking the best you can? There are many suggestions for specifically starting a new body improvement plan. I won't attempt to cover every inch, but with your good eyes and mind, you can take your own personal inventory now. Let's start from the top.

Hair

Is your hair becoming? Is it clean? Styles at the present time are "anything goes," so it's fun to be creative in finding the "real you."

Try a cut that looks nice and neat most of the week. Right after combing, certain styles may be stunning show-stoppers, but if ten minutes later they are sloppy shag-moppers, try something new.

Longer styles for men are very attractive, if their hair is clean and groomed. I like the mustache craze too, if it suits the man and the man trims the 'stache.

Complexion

This is a problem spot for some which usually

improves with age—to a certain point! If professional help is needed, by all means get it for health reasons as well as cosmetic. Acne, if untreated, can become a serious hazard with secondary infection causing bad scarring. Healthy skin comes from good living— plenty of good food, exercise and happiness.

Cosmetics can help or hinder. The "natural look" is great, and the assortments of expensive creams, lotions and gels may or may not be necessary. The plaster, china-doll face or heavy makeup looks as if it might crack any minute. I'm always a little uneasy around these people, afraid that they may smile or frown and cause major damage.

A good policy is to: (1) start with as little commercial help as possible; (2) evaluate; (3) redo, if necessary, perhaps adding a little color here and there; (4) and re-evaluate. Have a friend help who seems to have the knack of looking great without trying.

You may look your very best in your own natural skin glow. A Scandinavian friend keeps the art of nature's gift in her lovely complexion untouched, and it contributes beautifully to her total natural personality. Cosmetics, skillfully and discreetly applied, can prevent those of us not so blessed from having a drab, washed-out appearance.

Heavy makeup with four-inch lashes may be a real "cover-up," an attempt to hide from an unfriendly world. Men may use massive beards or mustaches as their camouflage. Both men and women may let their hair cover as much as possible—those jungle styles that make you wonder if you are talking to a pair of hidden eyes or the back of a head. Such tendencies tell the world that here maybe persons of deep insecurity.

61

Mouth

Unattractive teeth and breath have no place in our body-temples, and can be prevented. The mouth is a natural focal point in daily interactions and is important in all our interpersonal relationships.

A lovely, natural smile is refreshing to both its owner and observer, and should be a frequent expression. We are all drawn to those who radiate a sense of deep contentment, whose laughter is a warm overflow of a rich, satisfied life. Of course, this may take a bit of internal remodeling too!

A pleasant facial expression may initially, require a conscientious effort. I often find myself frowning, especially when in serious thought. It's true that it takes less physiological effort to smile. Retrain your facial muscles to relax. Be natural—and let the easiest route take over!

Voice tone and pitch are important too. Adjusting the volume is a good suggestion in most cases, without the extremes of soft, sickening cooing or loud, boisterous bellowing. High pitch for men and low pitch for women may be a hormonal problem, and may be improved by voice training. Severe abnormalities need medical attention and treatment.

Body

The head needs a body to belong to—and one that fits! Body types are unchangeable but a general redistribution is often possible. Exercise and weight control aren't easy, but then, steady discipline never is. I observe that when self-discipline slips in my diet, there is a coordinating lack in other areas of my life as well. Most of us would look and feel a hundred percent better if our bodies were in top shape.

I once labeled my campaign against flab, "Operation Skinny Ginny," and had fun setting weekly goals. Setbacks were far too frequent—and still are, but I'm convinced that when I look my best I feel terrific. Good literature on exercise and diet control is copious. Start your own campaign with realistic goals and see what a difference it makes.

Hands

Grooming may sound like a term for the stable, and many appear as if they had done theirs in the barn! Cleanliness isn't just the daily shower routine but may also take a little extra trimming around the edges. Along with your mouth, your hands are major focal points in social interactions, and should be attractive.

Nail care doesn't have to be an extravagant manicure, but trimmed, clean nails are prerequisite to good looks for both men and women. Nail polish varies with individual taste, as does nail length. The dagger quality of some nails, dripping blood red, are foreboding to me, as well as downright dangerous.

Clothes

Clothes also contribute to the well-groomed look. Clean, fresh, well-fitted garments give an extra sparkle to the temple-body we're working so hard to improve.

Clothes styles, like hair, vary with individual taste and it's hard to be out of style these days. I could wear my grandma's honeymoon outfit and look "in" during this crazy fashion era. But it is important to choose the most becoming look that's comfortable and within the limits of good taste.

Immodesty is unbecoming to royalty—remember we are heirs of God. But it isn't modest to hide behind a drab sack; rather, it's denying part of the loveliness that God created in you. A well-proportioned body should be complemented, not obscured, by its dress.

It is immodest to flaunt or reveal too much. King Solomon, famous for his wisdom and quite a connoisseur of lovely women, had this to say about immodesty, "As a ring of gold in a swine's snout, so is a beautiful woman who lacks discretion" (Prov. 11:22, *NASB*). Glitter in a pig's nose isn't much of a description of real beauty, is it.

Colors should be as abundant and bright as are those God has given us in the created world. Coordination of style, color and fit should produce a sense of "just right."

Femininity and masculinity have long been partially defined by dress. As we've discussed, it's a much deeper issue. But the trend toward unisex clothing is rather boring and disturbing. I still appreciate lace and frills now and then and would rather enjoy them on myself than on my date. Slacks for ladies are often more convenient, comfortable and modest, but can be tiresome if worn exclusively.

What is really important is not the dress itself, but the attitude of the wearer. A lady who is comfortable with herself and her sexuality can look elegant and feminine in the most tailored style. One who is not cannot disguise this lack even with the softest, most alluring style.

Individuality is the key with limits of modesty and refinement. Try new styles as an adventure. Men have never had such an exciting range before. The new casual look of no tie, open collar is great for some but the sharp, conventional look is still more attractive for others.

Enough about clothes—go on with your personal inventory until you reach the tip of your last toenail. Our appearance should give a total picture of pleasing looks, reflecting refinement and good character. No one feature should distract from another.

Many have said that our outward appearance is merely a frame for inner beauty. This is very true. And the most gorgeous frame cannot erase the ugliness of a selfish, shriveling soul. There is no substitute for inner loveliness, but it surely deserves a beautiful, complementary frame.

Beauty Spelled T-H-A-N-K Y-O-U

Self-acceptance of our outward appearance isn't an apathetic attitude of "Oh, well, I can't improve on nature." Many of us not only refuse to improve, but we hide or distort what is there. "Be the best you can be" in appearance pleases God; then to accept our appearance after we've made that genuine effort *is* important.

There are certain degrees of good looks in the standard of every culture and not many of us qualify as breath-taking beauties. To believe that God's creative work is good is difficult sometimes, especially when the "mirror, mirror on the wall" tells us we're not fair at all. But a genuine "thank you" for the body that God fashioned is necessary if we are to be truly attractive persons.

One of my men friends is by no means handsome if you analyze his features, complexion and body build. But he is honestly one of the most attractive, engaging people I know. He demonstrates his own self-acceptance by his warm receptivity to everyone he meets.

He displays initiative and drive while being very sensitive to those around him. He's consistently well-groomed and stylishly dressed. He has a quick wit and a warm sense of humor that makes one feel he is very comfortable with his looks.

An appealing person doesn't have to be gorgeous, but grateful. In acceptance of your appearance, thank God with an enthusiastic effort to be the best-looking temple possible.

Health Help

A major factor in our appearance, as well as our total well-being, is our health. Poor health not only makes us *look* like death warmed over, it makes us *feel* that way. Even in the young, vitality can fast fade if health is ignored.

A consistent failure to meet our body's minimum needs of nutrition, exercise and rest can one day explode into a full-scale breakdown and cause irreversible damage. In the meantime, we function at a sub-level of efficiency. Mental depression, fatigue, nervous tension, and fear all can result from below-par health.

Let me give you some specifics.

Nutrition

Everyone loves to eat—but few like to discuss nutrition. One college-age survey revealed that only 19 percent of those surveyed had what could be classified as good diets.[2] Busy schedules, convenience foods, working mothers, increasing food prices and a general lack of nutritional knowledge have contributed greatly to poor nutrition in recent years.

Snacking and omitting breakfast are two common bad habits. By one study the average college student consumes 513 calories a day in snacks—primarily candy and carbonated beverages.[3]

Extra moments of precious sleep often take precedence over a substantial breakfast. This results in a lowered performance, poor attitude and increased appetite during the remainder of the day.[4]

General poor nutrition ultimately will result in a higher susceptibility to disease, poor posture, fatigue, irritability, depression, nervousness, and inability to concentrate. Women not only harm themselves, but any children they may bear in the years to come.[5]

God created our bodies to operate on a certain mixture of fuel, and it's foolish not to follow instructions. The most common deficiencies seem to be protein, vitamins and iron. If your pep is pooped, analyze your daily intake and see if you lack any of these essentials.

Iron deficiency for women is very common, especially during menstruation. A good self-check for anemia is to lower your bottom eyelid and observe its inner color. If it's pale—hit the Geritol! A nice pink surface gives you a clean bill.

Daniel, as in the lion's den, certainly thought that nutrition was important. His experiment at Nebuchadnezzar's Cafeteria proved that eating right can surely pay off. Even the king noticed that "their countenances appeared fairer" (Dan. 1:15, *KJV*), after Daniel and his buddies stayed on a balanced diet for just ten days.

Try your own experiment of good eating for ten days. You might feel so terrific you won't recognize yourself ... and who knows who might notice that fairer countenance!

Sleep

"Natural sleep is the most satisfying form of recuperation from tension and fatigue."[6] Without a sufficient amount of sleep, recuperation is impossible. Tired tension is followed by lack of initiative, deep depression and finally physical and mental collapse.

The amount of sleep that is needed varies with the individual, with an average of the classic eight hours. People who tend to be nervous and tense require more than those with more placid dispositions. Determine your need and get it. Parents of young children may be screaming, "HOW?"

There's no substitute for a solid night's sleep, but short periods of rest during a busy day, perhaps only ten minutes listening to soothing music, may serve to relax and release tension.

God gave us one day out of seven as a respite from a tiring week, and it's a tremendous opportunity to catch up on lost rest. That's not just a suggestion—it's one of God's commands.

Experiment for a month and let every Sunday be the quietest, most relaxed day you can make it. Worship refreshes our bodies as well as our souls. See what a difference it will make. I found that when I didn't study on Sunday during college, I was far more efficient the rest of the week.

Exercise

Regular exercise also keeps the kinks out of our system. It's needed to tone our muscles and keep our bodies in maximum working order. Release of physical energy reduces nervous tension and promotes good appetite and restful sleep.

These are only basics of which most people are very aware. But it's startling to me the number of patients I care for who are ill because they failed to follow these basics. Check your health habits and see if they need improvement.

A thorough physical check-up is a good idea too—it's surely easier to prevent than to cure. Make sure your body is in maximum functioning order and help it stay that way.

A healthy, attractive body is part of God's best for us—it's part of what pleases Him. Our health as well as our appearance reflects how we view ourselves and life in general. For example, an overweight person may not like himself or the world, so he uses obesity as punishment.

Good health also enhances interpersonal relationships. Physical well-being promotes our intellectual capacity. Our relationship to God is certainly influenced by the temple we keep for Him.

Another topic that may associate with our physical well-being is the highly-charged subject of sex. The extent to which sexual drives are satisfied has long been proclaimed the sole determinate of health and happiness. We certainly have sexual desires and drives—stronger than many other basic needs. How should we handle them without their controlling us?

Footnotes

1. Excerpted from *Genesis in Space and Time* by Francis A. Schaeffer. © 1972 by L'Abri Fellowship, Switzerland, pg. 101. Used by permission of InterVarsity Press, USA.
2. C.B. Young and C.A. Storwick, "Food Habits of Freshmen at Oregon State College," quoted by Cleveland Hickman, *Health for College Students* (Englewood Cliffs, N.J.: Prentice Hall, Inc., 1968), p. 199.
3. Madge Myers, Elaine Sullivan, Fredrick Stace, "Foods Consumed by University Students" quoted by Jesse Williams, Angela Kitzinger, *Health for the College Student* (New York: Harper and Row, 1967), p. 152.
4. W.W. Tuttle, Katherine Daum, Ruth Larson, "Effect on School Boys: Omitting Breakfast," quoted by Miriam Tuck and Franklin Haar, *Health* (New York: Harper and Row, 1969), p. 77.
5. Miriam Tuck and Franklin Haar, *Health* (New York: Harper and Row, 1969), p. 78.
6. Cleveland Hickman, *Health for College Students* (Englewood Cliffs; N.J.: Prentice Hall, Inc., 1968), p. 130.

SIX
SEXUAL DEVELOPMENT:
SEX IS GOD'S IDEA

As always, sex remains a popular, relevant topic of discussion. And the current freedom from puritanical taboos is right.

But dialogues about sex are a dime a dozen these days, and that seems pretty cheap material to me. So I can't help but wonder if we've not lost something in the transition from "hush, hush" to "tell it like it is"—or more frequently, like it isn't!

We may be misusing our new-found freedom to openly explore this subject. For sex is an intensely personal affair and when it is divorced from that context by academic discussions, it becomes less than it was meant to be.

Physical oneness is so profoundly deep in its capacity to express total love that it goes far beyond our ability to explain the experience in mere words. Yet man, from the pulpit and platform, seeks to enlighten our inhibited psyches. But detailed confessions of dismal pasts or careful instruction of successful ways and means are out of place at public gatherings, even vulgar. The feeling tone of previous intimacy is lost.

Discretion in our converstaion is wise, but not because sex is anything less than pure. We should not swing to the other extreme of the Victorian age in fear of admitting natural desires and passion. We may find that sharing and exploring our thoughts and feelings about sex is very appropriate and needful. Misconceptions, distorted views and fears may need to be released and a happy, healthy attitude may come only after practical discussion with respected friends and professionals.

So, since our nature seems to rebel against balance, we are threatened in our discussion by two extremes. One extreme is to become wrongfully preoccupied so that we isolate sex from its intensely personal context and make dialogue an excuse to linger on lustful thought. The other extreme is to be wrongfully inhibited, to avoid the topic as less than pure and smother into repression our God-given sexual capacity. Both extremes are injurious, and I sincerely desire to hit middle ground.

Perfection or Distortion?

Stop a moment and think what comes to your mind with the word "sex." Be honest and examine how healthy your thinking is. "Healthy" may be defined as "freedom from defect or disease, soundness, absence of deviation from what is perfect." And we need this soundness of thinking long before the wedding bells.

Yet many of our attitudes toward sex and much of our behavior in this area are not healthy; they are defective, diseased, unsound and deviant from intended perfection. Distorted, devilish norms subconsciously invade our mental and emotional stance.

How? Why?

We are saturated with a diet of lustful propaganda.

It clogs our inner mental mechanisms with its grime. And, in time, our lives correspond with the compromised values we acquire and the warped experiences we are exposed to.

Note that I am not speaking of the degenerate, but everyday people, of myself. I need God to scrub my mind of the distortions I constantly see and hear.

While I was in Israel a few years ago, I was impressed by a remark from our Jewish guide. He pointed to a television antenna and said, "That's the devil's tail in my country!"

We need to remember that the devil's tail is long and that it flails everywhere. Here in America, no less than in Israel, our media is flooded with a twisted, almost savage perversion of the truth. Isn't it like our adversary to take such a thing of beauty and destroy it for so many?

My perspective is admittedly limited by my young, unmarried status. Nevertheless, I believe that many problems for both marrieds and unmarrieds could be solved if we recognize certain truths concerning God's design of our sexuality. So let's climb up and see our sexual capacity from His perspective.

It's an exciting view!

To understand all that sex was created and intended to be, and to make an effort to keep this perspective in a world which is constantly at war with the truth is imperative. This understanding is imperative if I am to live to my potential in the area of personal sexual development—whether I'm married or not.

One good anti-pollution program is to go back to that exciting love story in Genesis. Remember where we were when we last saw Mr. and Mrs. Adam? They were just getting acquainted. Adam had done some pretty heavy sleeping and awoke to a surprise garden party introducing Eve from Eden.

Eve, presented by the Creator Himself, was not bothered with the decision of which gown to wear for the occasion. Very reverently, Scripture gives a beautiful description of their introductory dress. "They were both naked, the man and his wife, and were not ashamed" (Gen. 2:25, *KJV*).

The origin of sex is in God's creative mind and man and woman freely enjoyed His design. Adam and Eve became "one flesh" without shame, guilt or embarrassment. In recognizing God's gift of one another they went on to fulfill that intended unity. Sex is part of perfect creation—it is good, declared God.

Man and woman were quite literally a part of each other in the method of creation—remember, removal of rib with major reconstruction. Very naturally, their original oneness was continued and enriched by sexual union with pure enjoyment at the wonder of God's design. God had fashioned a beautiful structural complement in His design of their bodies. But His purpose for complete sexual experience goes far deeper than just physical unity.

God intends that sex involve the complete innervation of the total person. It is to be a culmination, the ultimate expression of oneness in every dimension of life for two persons. God gives it to be freely and creatively appropriated by each couple in a growing, fruit-bearing relationship. Sex then is certainly not too "fleshly" to be holy and beautiful. Neither should it be viewed as too sacred to be fun.

Marrieds may sometimes fail to recognize the tremendous variability of their possession. Being sensitive and responsive to the moods and needs of each other, they can be very creative in sexual expression. A sacredness akin to worship may pervade one experience, while the next may be simple, playful, passionate fun. One is not less than the other—both are spiritual in the context that they are fulfilling what God intended in marriage.

A Time to Embrace

A familiar question that's always raised is, "Why must this beautiful expression of love be confined to marriage?" Yet God leaves no doubt in our minds that sex is lawfully limited to marriage.

"Don't you know that if a man joins himself to a prostitute she becomes part of him and he becomes part of her? For God tells us in Scripture that in His sight the two become one person. Don't you realize that your bodies are actually part of the members of Christ? So should I take part of Christ and join Him to a prostitute? Never!" (1 Cor. 6:15,16, *TLB*).

Sex outside of God's blessing in marriage is blasphemous against ourselves and God. The reason is found in the very nature of man himself. Deeply imbedded in the core of every personality is the intense desire to relate to another, completely. This relationship is to involve a mutual blending in every realm of life. Sex was given to fulfill that desire, to be a beautiful avenue of demonstrative expression of complete unity of body, soul and spirit.

Logically such a relationship, by its very nature, must be exclusive to one person. Otherwise, it becomes meaningless. Such intense, deep sharing can only be experienced in the permanent commitment of the marriage covenant. Any other context is in strenuous opposition to this depth of giving love.

God's purpose for forbidding pre- and extra-marital sex is not meant to restrict or limit our pleasure. Rather, his purpose is to provide maximum fulfillment—to give His best in this total relationship.

I enjoyed teaching water skiing last summer in the beautiful Adirondack mountains of New York. And I can see in the clear, cold waters of those gorgeous lakes, an illustration of the intent of God's instructions concerning sex.

To learn to ski, my pupils had to know and follow the rules. Funny, but I never had one refuse to wear the skis or insist that he didn't need the boat. After he learned the correct position for take-off and the skill of maintaining balance, the experience was fun and exhilarating.

A few more independent souls who insisted on pulling against the boat, or who bent their arms to take up slack, soon found themselves several feet under. They never shouted their right or freedom to do things their own way as they came gulping to the surface with their skis around their necks. They soon realized that following rules didn't limit their liberty to ski—but defined it!

That, simply, is what God has done in His instructions concerning the context of sexual experience. He made us a certain way and wants us to enjoy sex completely, as He intended—in marriage.

To reduce sex to a physical act with some emotional overtones is sadly to sag to a low level of existing as sophisticated beasts. To elevate sex to the beauty of mutual, total commitment is to expectantly strive toward God's highest in kingly pleasure.

Isn't it just like God to provide such a delight, such joy for His children? And, isn't it just like us to misuse such a gift, robbing ourselves of the maximum pleasure that God planned?

It's never too late to ask God to heal our sick hearts and minds and restore health to our perspective and behavior. Rahab, a professional in sexual sin, experienced such restoration. She even gained a position as a champion of faith in the book of Hebrews' Hall of Fame (Heb. 11:31). God's forgiveness is complete with "No condemnation."

There may be battle scars, but we are never at the mercy of our pasts. Satan delights to thrust before us our failures and flood our minds with guilt and regret. He taunts that we don't deserve anything good because we've been so bad. When he is no longer successful in his temptation, Satan will render us spiritually impotent by memories of defeat. This is true to those within as well as without marriage.

God has a different approach to our past. Not only does He declare us forgiven, but He challenges:

"Strip yourselves of your former nature ... your previous manner of life ... lusts and desires that spring from delusion. Be constantly renewed in the spirit of your mind—having a fresh mental and spiritual attitude" (Eph. 4:22,23, *Amplified*).

Claim this clean record and start living in God's highest as a sexual being.

Sexuality—Develop It Now

Sex is not the center of marriage, but it is important. Consequently, developing individual sexual potential within marriage is also important and should not be underrated. For if either partner is frustrated or dissatisfied, complete harmony in other areas of living is difficult.

Serious sexual incompatibility, however, is not just a problem in itself, but a symptom of more serious underlying problems. Marrieds encountering such problems should realize there's much helpful literature available written by godly authorities who are expert on the subject and should investigate this material. Open communication with honest admission of feelings is a good place to begin toward resolution of sexual incompatibility.

And how does one develop personal sexual potential without marriage? Since un-marriage is my present state, the answer to that question concerns me as well as you. First of all, let's recognize that experimentation—in any sense of that term—is out. "Fooling around" with high explosives is never wise!

Uncontrolled release of sexual drive, apart from a permanent mutual commitment, can only lead to disappointment, guilt and perhaps even frigidity or impotence. Abstinence won't!

Sexual techniques can be easily learned, and what a joy for two people to enter that school together for the first time as man and wife. On such a basis, there's no struggle to compete or match educations, no need to hide or forget past memories.

It is neither smart nor clever to misuse God's gift of sex and then miss the highest and best He has for us. And since God clearly forbids sex outside of marriage, the first way to develop sexual potential for marriage is to wait until marriage to experiment.

But there's another way to develop our sexuality as unmarrieds. And this we can do in preparation for marriage—after all, it's still God's norm—or even if we remain unmarried.

And what is this other way?

First, we learn to see sex from God's perspective— as a total union of persons. Then we concentrate on developing those other essentials, apart from the physical union, that will lead to a complete, harmonious, satisfying relationship.

We can begin the process by learning to feel tones before marriage. In fact, we must begin before marriage. Self-acceptance, open communications patterns, sensitivity, responsiveness and unselfish love lead the list of priorities. And these alone should keep any unmarried busy enough to stay out of mischief!

These qualities, if integrated into one's life, are infallible in their ability to produce an attractive, admired person in the present tense. At the same time, these qualities prepare a person to be an exciting, satisfying lover if the future brings marriage. If not, this individual will be valued and loved for his ability to be a friend to members of the same and the opposite sex.

Walter Trobisch in *I Loved a Girl*, a remarkable record of his private correspondence with two young Africans, gives this emphasis:

"It is good, Francois, that you want to prepare yourself for marriage. But what is most important here is not the physical functioning of the sex organs. What matters is the psychological adjustment—in other words, the meeting of the hearts and minds of two partners.

"Have you ever heard an orchestra tune its instruments before a concert? First comes the oboes, the violins, and the flutes. If the conductor started with the trumpets and drums which make a great deal of noise, he wouldn't be able to hear the oboes, violins, and flutes. It's the same in the orchestra of marriage.

The adjustment of heart and mind correspond to the tuning of woodwinds and strings, then later the drums and trumpets of sex can be sounded."[1]

Touch Control

Practically, where does all this lead our personal convictions of morals and standards? Strong desires and drives are still part of our makeup. They cannot be denied and repression isn't what God wants; those drives are a part of the way He made us—they are good, right and beautiful. But He does want us to learn to handle them. Even after marriage, with inevitable sickness or separation, such self-control is necessary. Before marriage, this tremendous source of energy should neither be denied nor unleashed, but rather channeled into creative outlets.

I'm not talking about the old cold shower, run-around-the-block routine. Physical exertion may release tension and at times is needful. But since part of our sexual drive is the desire to meaningfully relate to another, one excellent channel to release that energy is active involvement with people.

Recognizing then this vital need for active personal involvement with others, what should be our standards of conduct toward the opposite sex? Personal convictions here should come not only from "what is right?" but also from "What is wise?" "What will enhance or contribute toward developing desired qualities of a total relationship between me and a member of the opposite sex?"

To become physically involved with another person can quickly gain preeminence and stifle other important essentials of a total relationship. Nonverbal expression of closeness—too much and too soon

—can rob the ability to verbally communicate. Such a relationship is confusing to both the man and the woman. The man will find it extremely difficult to distinguish between unselfish love and selfish desire; the woman is insecure as to what is most valuable—a desirable body or the real, inside person.

For a couple to decide to marry at this stage of the game is mighty shaky. Wouldn't it be wiser to avoid physical involvement until after a commitment is made? Such a permanent decision as marriage deserves a solid foundation of mutual knowledge of the basic persons involved and not just the level of hormones each one arouses.

Physical expression of affection and passion seem to be as natural as breathing. To limit such expression is never easy. The first step is *to sincerely desire to please God in this area of our lives.* A verse that has been a standard reminder in my life is, "Let integrity and uprightness preserve me; for I wait on thee" (Ps. 25:21, *KJV*). God will define that level of "integrity and uprightness" to you personally if you trust Him and seek it.

The next step is *to avoid situations that strongly shake the standard that God has given.* We are, many times, like the little guy who took his swimming suit to the pond after his mother forbade him to go swimming. He wanted to be prepared just in case he got tempted and fell in. If we are indiscriminate with whom we associate and where we associate, we'll surely have a tough time with the "how far."

Standards of modesty shouldn't stop with dress; modesty is more of an inner attitude than an outward appearance. A person can be wrongfully provocative in the most conservative dress. Check how much you are willfully tempting the standards that you have claimed. "I just couldn't help it" is never a good excuse.

Touching isn't wrong—it's basic in the world of human relationships. We demonstrate warm affection when we cuddle a baby, hug or kiss family members or friends on special occasions. Such expressions are almost automatic and we all have different patterns learned from our backgrounds. My family tends to be champion huggers! Such expressions of affection seem naturally appropriate to close friends of the opposite sex on occasion.

A sensible standard may be: physical expression that is appropriate for family and for friends of the same sex is also appropriate with those friends of the opposite sex. For without a genuine interest in the total person, other physical expression becomes superficial and selfish.

It's often hard to distinguish between warm affection and passion. Even the so-called "harmless goodnight kiss" can carry some mighty strong messages. Not that passion is wrong; God made us that way, and it provides a beautiful mode of fulfillment in the permanence of marriage.

But before a commitment is made toward marriage, why start something with neither promise nor freedom to finish? I anticipate loving my husband so completely that I want to honor and respect myself for him now. But it is not merely a question of "saving yourself," but rather one of enjoying the depth of person-centered, total relationship now, without defrauding and without provoking unfulfilled desires.

Again, God will define that level of "integrity and

uprightness," of what is truly wise, to you personally, if you trust Him and seek it.

Much of what we learn seems to come the hard way, through experiences that hurt and disappoint, but still teach. Yet we are never left to muddle our way blindly out of past pits of failure. We can begin now— this moment—to reach toward God's highest in developing our sexual potential. Purposeful, serious commitment to personal purity and unselfish involvement with others is a tremendous start in the right direction.

This kind of person may be rightfully called "sensuous." Gladys Hunt in *Ms. Means Myself* comments: "Sensuous is a word that needs to be rescued from purely sexual connotations. To be sensuous means to be present in every moment of life—feeling life, enjoying it, learning, exploring, appreciating the world God made and the people in it."[2]

The following poem written by Michel Quoist in his book, *Prayers*, is a poignant cry of a young man's heart:

"I want to love, Lord,
   I need to love.
   All my being is desire;
   My heart,
   My body
      yearn in the night towards
      an unknown one to love.
   My arms thrash about,
      and I can seize on no object for my love.
   I am alone and want to be two.
   I speak, and no one is there to listen.
   I live, and no one is there to share my life.

Why be so rich and have no one to enrich?
Where does this love come from?
Where is it going?
I want to love, Lord,
I need to love.
Here this evening, Lord,
  is all my love, unused.

Listen, son,
Stop, and make, silently, a long pilgrimage
  to the bottom of your heart.
Walk by the side of your love so new,
  as one follows a brook to find its source,
And at the very end, deep within you,
  in the infinite mystery of your troubled soul,
  you will meet me.
For I call myself Love, son,
And from the beginning I have been nothing
  but Love, and Love is in you.

It is I who made you to love,
  To love eternally;
And your love will pass
  through another self of yours—
It is she that you seek:
Set your mind at rest; she is on your way,
  on the way since the beginning,
  the way of my love.
You must wait for her coming.
She is approaching,
You are approaching.
You will recognize each other,
For I've made her body for you,
  I've made yours for her.

I've made your heart for her,
  I've made hers for you,
And you seek each other, in the night,
  In "my night,"
Which will become Light if you trust me.

Keep yourself for her, son,
  As she is keeping herself for you.
I shall keep you for one another,
And since you hunger for love,
  I've put on your way
  all your brothers to love.
Believe me,
  It's a long apprenticeship, learning to love,
And there are not several kinds of love:
Loving is always leaving oneself
  to go towards others . . . .

Lord, help me to forget myself for others,
  My brothers, that in giving myself
  I may teach myself to love."[3]

Yes, I *do* believe in premarital love!

Footnotes

1. Walter Trobisch, *I Loved a Girl* (New York: Harper and Row Publishers, 1964), pp. 6,7.
2. Gladys Hunt, *Ms. Means Myself* (Grand Rapids, Mich.: Zondervan Publishing House, 1972), p. 109.
3. Michel Quoist, "To Love: The Prayer of the Adolescent," *Prayers* (New York: Sheed and Ward, Inc., 1963), pp. 52,53.

SEVEN
EMOTIONAL DEVELOPMENT: PREMARITAL LOVE IS GREAT!

"We're not sure of the future yet, whether we will marry, but Virginia, I really love him. I care deeply about what is happening in his life. I am learning to care more and more. Is it right for me to feel that way when I'm not sure that he's the man I will marry?" Dorothy's face was radiant with evident love as she shared these feelings with me. But with her last question a troubled frown crept into that glow.

My reply went something like this, "Dorothy, I've learned that I *never* lose when I really love. I may make myself vulnerable to all sorts of hurt ... but I never lose. Nor does it leave me with less of my heart to give to another, perhaps one other, exclusively someday.

"Instead it creates a greater capacity to love and be loved. Love is something we'll never learn enough about on this side of time and space. I'm thankful for every opportunity I have to learn!"

I wasn't advocating premature promises or extensive physical involvement. Neither are necessary to love. Both may be serious handicaps to the outworking of the love of God in us. If such love is learned first, both promise of commitment and physical expression will have solid significance.

The Will of Love

Love may be recognized by our emotions but it does not originate there. It is rooted in our wills. Remember that before love can have any meaning there must be a choice.

God chose to love us, and He gives us the option to respond to that love, just as He did for Adam and Eve. He gives every individual, every "single" the option to respond to His love. This is one thing that makes Christianity uniquely profound in the multitude of noble philosophies and religions.

Man does not have to reach God by ritual or intense meditation. God has already taken the initiative by reaching toward man with giving love.

A.W. Tozer comments,

"It is a strange and beautiful eccentricity of the free God that He allowed His heart to be emotionally identified with men. Self-sufficient as He is, He wants our love, and will not be satisfied until He gets it . . . . Free as He is, He has let His heart be bound to us forever . . . . True Christian joy is the heart's harmonious response to the Lord's song of love."[1]

God's love for us is not motivated by any inner need, but from "plenteousness that desires to give."[2]

"Love ever gives, forgives, outlives;
  And ever stands with open hands.
  For while love gives, it lives;
  And while love lives, it gives.
  Yea, this is love's prerogative
  To give—and give—and give."[3]

Much of what is tossed around today as "true luv" is a disappointing mirage that quickly fades. Its theme is not giving, but to get and get and get again.

One of the students at the university was describing to me how very much in love she was with a certain fellow. She admitted that he wasn't the most "lawful soul" at times but she loved him anyway. She exclaimed, "He makes me feel so good when I'm with him—like a real woman. That really turns me on. He gives me the kind of admiration I need."

"Is what you can give him more important to you than what he gives you?" I asked.

Her silence was her answer.

God wants a higher level of giving-love to penetrate our lives—a love refined of selfishness. The *motive* of such love is to give, not to receive. Yet beautifully, the *result* of such love is to receive in unimagined abundance.

It seems a paradox, doesn't it? I do not love in order to delight myself, but when I love unselfishly I cannot escape this delight. It's just God's happy order of love. For the very nature of love is that it takes pleasure in its object.

"Jehovah thy God is in the midst of thee, a mighty One who will save (giving, giving, giving), He will rejoice over thee with joy; He will rest in His love; He will joy over thee with singing (delighting, delighting, delighting)" (Zeph. 3:17, *ASV*). This makes our one objective in life, "to please God's heart," both an appropriation and a fulfillment of His giving love. Only God can teach us this quality of love.

"What the World Needs Now Is Love, Sweet Love" or "Love Makes the World Go Round" are catchy song titles. I'm sure they were never written to be profoundly spiritual statements, but they do express truth. Love is the central turning, motivating force in a satisfied life.

Our present civilization may suggest many other solutions to individual and corporate security and peace. People are forever searching for the missing element in their lives and they draw near to the true Source as they seek to love and be loved. But the clever counterfeit "lust" too frequently is substituted for love and it is never quite enough.

Children are the world's best teachers and through their transparent honesty we learn much. I had an experience with a child recently that illustrates the need and the real meaning of love.

It happened as I was tucking sweet niece Mary in bed for the night. She begged me to stay a moment and asked with unusual seriousness, "Aunt Virginia, was there something that you always wanted and couldn't think what it was?"

"Do you mean a toy, or something to eat?" I inquired.

"No," she sighed, "I don't think so. It's just *something*—I wish I knew what it was. If I had it, I just know I'd be happy. I think maybe it's that I need to play and have more fun—have fun all the time."

How descriptive of the yearning emptiness of ego-centric living! All children must learn that the center of the world is not themselves. Do some of us *ever* learn that?

I was so moved that night by Mary's comment, knowing that she had been growing in her understanding of God's love and forgiveness in recent months, that I responded with this explanation.

"Yes, it's nice to have fun, Mary. But that's not really what makes us happy. Making people who love you happy is the most fun of all. God loves you and when you obey Him it makes Him happy. Your mommy and daddy love you and when you obey them, it makes them happy. When you disobey, it hurts God and your mommy and daddy—and are you very happy?"

"No, ma'am," was her solemn reply.

"I began to learn that truth when I was just about your age, Mary. The more I did to make other people happy, the happier I became. God helps us to obey. He helps us to be unselfish. He helps us to really love Him and others, in the same way that He loves us.

"Giving becomes more important to us than getting. That's when we are the happiest. Do you understand?"

"Yes, I think so," she quietly nodded.

I gave her a warm hug and kiss and assured her, "I love you very much, Mary. Your mommy and daddy do too. God does too—He wants you to be happy."

Prayerfully I left her, trusting God to give her understanding.

Evidence of her understanding came on my birthday. Her parents had already arranged a gift from Mary to me and it was appreciated. But dear little Mary had plans of her own. She excitedly presented me four of her treasured pennies, carefully wrapped in a tissue, with a scrawled "I love you" on top.

She wanted to demonstrate her love by giving something that was important to her, a part of herself. How I cherished that gift of her unselfish love! What a joy to watch her happy, exuberant face as she presented her sacrifice.

The Fear to Love

We need to learn to love, to learn how to love. But first we must open ourselves to learn. For many reasons we fear to love, and to be loved. We are like the child who desperately wants to swim, yet refuses to go near the water for fear of drowning. Psychologists tell us, "It's one of the most puzzling facts of human existence, that we often avoid the very experience we most desire."[4]

We fear vulnerability, disappointment, hurt. We remember betrayed confidences, broken promises, indifferent responses to our attempts to love. It's much easier to withdraw and prevent further injury than to risk another hurt.

During such a period of hurt, I found this passage by C.S. Lewis in his book, *The Four Loves*. It challenged my fear of loving again:

"There is no safe investment. To love at all is to be vulnerable. Love anything and your heart will certainly be wrung and possibly be broken.

"If you want to make sure of keeping it intact, you must give your heart to no one, not even an animal. Wrap it carefully round with hobbies and little luxuries; avoid all entanglements; lock it up safe in the casket or coffin of your selfishness. But in that casket, safe, dark, motionless, airless—it will change. It will not be broken—it will become unbreakable, impenetrable, irredeemable . . . .

"We shall draw nearer to God, not by trying to avoid the sufferings inherent in all loves, but by accepting them and offering them to Him, throwing away all defensive armour. If our hearts need to be broken, and if He chooses this as the way in which they should break, so be it."[5]

God, in His perfect goodness and love, never causes pain. A broken heart comes as a result of living in a broken world of broken people and we all suffer from it at one time or another. Yet God may make use of pain as a tutor of love.

When disappointment and disillusionment give us opportunity to respond, our involuntary emotional reactions tend to be quite honest. We may see clearly that our motives and attitudes in the whole affair weren't too unselfish after all. This gives God the opportunity to purify our love and make us desire only the best for the one we love.

This is one of the most thrilling, enriching processes in life—I know it to be true! I experienced a deep level of joy when a man I loved very much married someone else after he realized it was God's best for him. My genuine joy at his happiness wasn't from some magnanimous self-sacrifice of my own; but was a result of God's refining work in my love for him. It was God's miracle, not my own strength.

Part of our fear to love and be loved, comes from our inability to accept ourselves. Emotional intimacy necessitates an honest level of sharing. Distrust of what we are really like, apart from our outward facade, may keep us from this involvement.

If we don't love ourselves, we will never be able to accept the fact that anyone else could possibly love us. We build walls to guard our fears and self-rejection, yet, we are still quite uncomfortable with ourselves within the inner court of those walls. We don't understand ourselves and what we do understand, we don't like.

Such individuals are not always the isolated, hermit type. Many use activity to escape the loneliness of their inner insecurity and fear. The ultra-busy, hyperactive go-getter may very well be using his schedule as bricks in his wall of seclusion. He may even have a wide scope of personal involvements in terms of "ministry."

Yet, apart from the function of helping, he cannot share himself. It's tragic to see such a person, giving everything he can in terms of effort and energy to anyone he thinks needs his help—everything except what is most needed and wanted . . . himself.

This attitude isn't part of God's highest for us. He longs to bring depth into our interpersonal relationships. He wants to teach us giving love and help us release our fears.

The Freedom to Love

Without giving love, our whole emotional stability is threatened. Giving love produces a healthy environment for all of our other emotions. Without it, fear, loneliness, depression, anger, hatred, and guilt have easy access and can dominate our worlds.

Giving love does not eliminate negative feelings entirely, but it does provide a means to cope with them. It welcomes joy, peace, security, patience and forms a cooperation with them to rule our lives.

Dr. Donald Grey Barnhouse makes this comment on the familiar verses, Galatians 5:22,23: "Love is the key. Joy is love singing. Peace is love resting. Long-suffering is love enduring. Kindness is love's habit. Gentleness is love's self-forgetfulness. Self-control is love holding the reins."[6]

If we choose to love, we can begin accepting ourselves as we accept someone we love. We learn much about ourselves in the process, about our capacity for selfishness, about how we manipulate others for our own convenience. We will also be astonished at the capacity that God gives us to begin reaching out to others, to become genuinely involved in their lives.

As we choose to love we will learn much of others. Love makes another person's feelings, ideas, problems, hopes, frustration more important than our own. To understand and share a life other than our own is never, ever wasted energy. If our perspective of life consists only of what we experience, we will have narrow, shallow vision. Deeper insight of the "real world" of real people can only come as we share ourself, by giving love.

Perhaps the most difficult context in which to develop this quality of love is within the relationship between a man and woman. Because men and women are intended to complete—to complement one another, there is a greater motivating need to develop giving love between them. However, each one of us is tempted to be selfish, possessive and jealous and we often become so preoccupied in meeting our own inner need, that giving of unselfish love is difficult.

All marriages should be prefaced by this quality of love, but all such love may not necessarily lead to marriage. Nor do all friendships involve this depth of love. Its specialness is reserved for a very few.

I believe my friend Dorothy, whom we met earlier, is experiencing the beauty of just such a relationship. She told me, "Whether I will ever be his wife really isn't the most important thing to me. I want to be to him what he needs now. I want to support him, pray for him, be sensitive as to how I can help him. God will take care of the future. In the meantime, I don't want to miss His best for us now."

She need not fear that her love for this man is wrong. To me, it's beautiful—a gracious unselfishness of heart that is a reflection of God's love in her life. If she marries this fellow, who seems to love her in the same way, what a marriage it will be! If not, they both will have grown in their knowledge of love, in their depth of sensitivity, responsiveness and un-selfishness to others.

The Mind of Love

There's an interesting contrast in Scripture as to what is taught concerning love and wisdom. Carefully compare these passages:

WISDOM	LOVE
(James 3:17, *ASV*)	
"But the wisdom that is from above is first . . .	
pure	" . . . love out of a *pure* heart and a good conscience and faith unfeigned." 1 Timothy 1:5 (*ASV*)
	"This love of which I speak of is . . .
	• slow to lose patience
	• looks for a way of being constructive
	• not possessive
peaceable	• not anxious to impress
gentle	• nor does it cherish

95

easy to be entreated full of mercy	inflated ideas of its own importance • has good manners • does not pursue selfish advantage • not touchy • does not keep account of evil or gloat over the wickedness of other people." 1 Corinthians 13:4-6 (*Phillips*)
full of good fruits	"But the fruit of the Spirit is *Love*, joy, peace, longsuffering, kindness, goodness, faithfulness, meekness, self-control." Galatians 5:22,23 (*ASV*)
without variance	"Love knows • no limit to endurance • no end to its trust • no fading of its hope It can outlast anything. It is, in fact, the one thing that still stands when all else has fallen." 1 Corinthians 13:7,8 (*Phillips*)
without hypocrisy	"Let love be without hypocrisy" Romans 12:9 (*ASV*)

96

There appears to be a close relationship between the two, doesn't there? Paul says there is (Phil. 1:9, *KJV*): "That your *love* may abound more and more with *knowledge* and all *discernment.*"

Could we then say that wisdom is to be the "mind" of love?

We've defined love as choosing what is right and best for the beloved . . . this necessitates wisdom. This gives stability to our changeable emotional natures. Real love is not dependent on our changing moods. Rather, it is deeply rooted in our wills and in the wisdom of our minds . . . it is "without variance."

We, as individuals, as "singles," can begin learning this quality of love in our lives. It defines our emotional potential. What a difference it will make in our lives, married or unmarried!

Wisdom may be defined as seeing life from God's perspective. Living life from God's perspective is LOVE!

_____

Love, we've learned, needs an object. People are the best targets I know . . . all kinds of people. Let's talk about them.

Footnotes

1. A.W. Tozer, *The Knowledge of the Holy* (New York: Harper and Brothers, 1961), pp. 107,109.
2. C.S. Lewis, *The Four Loves* (New York: Harcourt Brace Jovanovich, Inc., 1960), p. 175.
3. J. Sidlow Baxter, *Going Deeper* (Grand Rapids, Mich.: Zondervan Publishing House, 1959), p. 143.
4. Marshall Bryant Hodge, *Your Fear of Love* (Garden City, N.Y.: death warrant of their relationship.
5. C.S. Lewis, *op cit., pp. 169,170.*
6. Dr. Donald Grey Barnhouse (source unknown)

EIGHT
SOCIAL DEVELOPMENT: IT'S WHO YOU KNOW THAT COUNTS

One of the most delightful, enlightening authors I know is Ethel Barrett. Here's an interesting portion of her "Advice to People Bumpers":

"The old axiom that 'solitude is often the best company' is true if you heed the word 'often' or even change it to 'sometimes' and don't take solitude across the board as the answer to everything. For in solitude we can develop everything but character. We can achieve much learning, stuff our heads with theory, learn the art of meditation, and yes, even become more spiritual—but it is only by bumping into other people that we develop character."[1]

This contact sport of "people-bumping" isn't easy, no matter what position you play. A married bumper with mate and children, has his own built-in team. Fussy babies, tired husbands and nervous wives can all add up to strike one, strike two, double play . . . home ruin! My married friends, between aspirins, tell me it's "all worth it," and I believe them—most of the time.

One of my fleeting moments of doubt came today as a friend, a mother of small children, collapsed after three days of sleepless travel. She didn't need great spiritual counsel or words of wisdom. She just needed a breather after more than her share of bumping. I marveled as she later gathered her crew, for the last leg of their journey, with quiet determination and more patience than I could have mustered. That takes character . . . and unselfish love.

Bumping isn't so easy for us unmarried folk, at times. The most frequent social scene is with our peers, those who share the same position along life's spectrum. These friendships seem to fall into two distinct categories—those with the same sex and those with the opposite. I'm not sure that they should be all that distinct within the context of friendship.

Courtship is, of course, different—but far richer when preceded by a sincere, open friendship. Yet, all too often open friendship is prevented by suspicion, jealousy, possessiveness—just plain old selfishness.

Dateline

Let's look at relationships between the sexes first. Casual, everyday contacts are difficult for some men and women, especially among the more "eligibles." "How do I meet men (or women)?" and "What do I do when I do meet them?" aren't uncommon questions.

For several years in my profession I worked with women, taught with women, lived with women—I actually began feeling a little strange around men, what little I saw of them. So, I began to overreact in fear that friendliness may be mistaken for the despised image of the "female on the hunt." I went to an extreme of aloofness, which was only a symptom of my insecurity and suspicion. One good friend confessed that his first impression was that I was the most conceited person he'd ever seen, and I'm afraid that's exactly how I acted. Such an attitude is not becoming to me or to the One I represent.

There is a balance somewhere between being a flirt and a snob. I'm not sure I can define it, but I do know that God can work it into my relationships, giving real personal freedom. God wants to free me from my self-consciousness in meeting people. He is doing some internal remodeling of my attitudes in the process. The more person-centered my social perspective becomes and the more God-centered my satisfaction becomes, the less inhibited and more balanced my interactions are.

Courtesy should prevail in all our relationships, including those between the sexes. One translation of 1 Corinthians 13:5 states "love has good manners." The sweeping, bowing, almost saluting of some more knightly-type gentlemen is a little overdone, I admit. I feel the most comfortable, the most "womanly" around fellows who appear most unaware of their natural consideration and courtesy.

Women need to learn to expect, to accept graciously and return such courtesy. I smile as I say that such lessons may not come without pain. Just last week I expected a large glass door to be held open for me and nearly lost my nose in the process of learning it wasn't. Several days later, not to be foiled again, I independently opened my own car door and promptly slammed it shut on my own hand. Some weeks you just can't win! After a broken thumb, lots of sympathy and a kind lecture, I've decided that expecting and waiting—with *caution*—for a gentleman's courtesy is best.

There are probably good books on dating etiquette on the market and many of us could use some good advice. Perhaps the most difficult task for the men is asking for a date—not asking doesn't take a lot of cleverness.

Women have a problem knowing how to decline graciously—"I'd love to" is simple. Trite phrases aren't the answer and often it's not the words that are said anyway, but the way they are spoken that matters. Everyone has his own style of expression, but the content should always be courteous and honest.

"Whatcha doing Friday night?" isn't appreciated by most women. It either traps them or leaves them feeling, "Well, if I'm not doing anything better, I may as well go out with him."

Some version of, "Would you be interested in going to dinner with me Friday night?" or "I'd like to take you to the game Saturday; would you be interested?" seems nicer.

One of the most tempting occasions for the "little white lie" comes when a girl wants to say no, and say it kindly. One good friend, now happily married, once told a persistent caller in desperation that she couldn't accept the date because, "The Lord might return before then!" That's *not* a suggestion, by the way!

There's no easy answer, but something like a simple, "No, thank you" or "I'd rather not" may be sufficient. A genuine "but I appreciate your invitation" or "thank you so much for calling" seems appropriate.

Long, detailed explanations need not be offered. Of course, it's not all so clear-cut and precise as these little phrases—two flesh-and-blood people with emotions and egos are involved. But again, there's no exception to kindness and honesty.

Different cultures have varied methods of matchmaking, with America's dating custom gaining popularity around the world. One particular incident, which has since become a family joke, really increased my appreciation of freedom of choice:

During a visit to Bethlehem, an Arab approached my dad and inquired of my parentage. My father luckily claimed me, to which claim our turbaned friend countered with an offer, "I'll give you twenty camels for her."

Startled, my dad shook his head and received one final offer, "I'll throw in five dogs."

That certainly did wonders for my sense of worth that day! What's worse is that Father hasn't had a better offer since!

Dating for the purpose of companionship and growing to know each other is great. But the popular collection of "games people play" in the dating scene doesn't promote that purpose.

One game is to look at every date only as a potential candidate for marriage—reducing dating to little more than a matrimonial shopping-spree. We need not conclude that a person should date anyone and everyone that comes along. Personal preferences are perfectly legitimate and many times it's kinder in the long run to avoid initial involvement. But there's much to be missed if our dating focus narrows itself to marriage possibilities.

Close, mutual relationships for right now are valuable environments for unselfish, person-centered love! However, a prevalent problem with these "healthy friendships" is the development of unequal aspirations. One may vote "yea" for a more permanent commitment, and the other "nay," with a plea for "just good friends." This is never an easy situation and the understanding between the two must be as individual as each of the participants.

Hurt is inevitable, but I wonder if it's not worsened by unnecessary wounded pride. Saying "no" to marriage may not negate the presence of deep respect, admiration and even love, but it may mean that the needed complement of total persons is just not there. It's a beautiful, special friendship that can graciously accept that truth and continue to be valued.

For other individuals, a mutual agreement to end contact without bitterness may be better. There's no easy formula for terminating a relationship that has had romantic overtones. Honesty is essential, but without cruel frankness.

I'll never forget the pain of one close Christian friend when a fellow to whom she was nearly engaged sent a sudden letter of cold rejection. He was honest all right: "I've burned your letters and pictures and hope you will do the same. I desire no further contact with you." But he was neither kind nor fair to her in his written death warrant of their relationship.

If a friendship has been serious enough to consider permanence, termination should be a face-to-face affair, when feasible. I'm certainly guilty of taking the easier "Dear John" escape, and deeply regret any hurt it's caused.

Whatever be the route of agreement, it should be mutually definite and clear. The "fading away" routine may on the surface appear kinder than confrontation, but perpetual uncertainty is much harder.

Our emotions, by nature, vacillate even in the best of relationships. When uncertainty and ambiguity govern communication or silence, we are in danger of weakening our emotional stability. During these times, we can say without spiritual idealism that God can be our Rock.

The knowledge of His goodness and sovereignty is a solid foundation in the midst of frustrating uncertainty that strives to pull us under. But this doesn't in any way excuse us from responsibility to one another. In all of our relationships, we need to be honest, be kind and be definite.

Dating can be the great American pastime of "how to waste money and avoid getting to know one another as persons." Creative dating can resolve matters in both areas here, as well as being an interesting project in itself. The most enjoyable times are most often the occasions where spontaneity reigns with lots of person-to-person communication. I find personally that casual, more natural settings always make me more comfortable and freer to be me.

Because many times the simple pleasures are the best, creative dating can really help on the financial end of things. Hiking, all-day bike rides and other sports, for example, are economical fun for the more out-door types. Others enjoy visiting interesting sites —museums, parks, gardens. I even remember one unique afternoon reading tombstones!

Try reading a book together and exchanging impressions. Get to know each other in real life situations. Enjoy children together or make a visit to some elderly friend. If possible, spend time with each other's families. You can find out much about a person by the way he interacts with home folk!

Do ask God to give both of you wisdom to know each other. After all, God's norm of companionship is for all men and women. A creative, unselfish approach to dating will contribute in reaching our potential of this norm.

Friendships with members of one's own sex can also provide rich companionships. Yet the David-Jonathan quality of such relationships is often prevented by pettiness, possessiveness and, again, just plain old selfishness. For an absorbing friendship that requires constant confirmation of its value and is frequently and easily hurt isn't healthy, nor does it involve giving-love.

The giving-love of true friends is freely unassuming and does not require a quota of attention, time and favor. Such a heart attitude doesn't demand loyalty, but commands trust. There's something uniquely releasing about sharing experiences with one who understands on the same genetic and hormonal level.

Be a People Person

Peer relationships are great, but we need to develop a total view of the human experience. It's often difficult to understand and accept those at different positions along life's spectrum. Accomplishing this understanding isn't through studying developmental theories or memorizing Erikson's eight stages of life. True understanding and appreciation for others come only as we become acquainted and involved with others who are in different stages of life than we are.

Children

It's delightful to learn to look through the eyes of a child. They have a "joy of the moment" enthusiasm that might be contagious if we would let ourselves be exposed. Parents have more than their share of such energetic vitality, I'm sure.

How easily we forget what it was like to be a little person with adults ordering our existence. A refresher course of spending time with children can never bring the same perspective again—but it will teach us much about life.

Children can be profound in their observations. They are usually uninhibited and can be bluntly honest in their evaluations. The simplicity and purity of a child's trusting heart is a model that Jesus used to teach His more mature followers.

I remember fondly one little doll, age 8-1/2, who rebuked my more sophisticated "practical" faith. Jennifer bounced into ski class one day with a resolute announcement, "I learned a Bible verse in class today, and I've decided to make a practical application to my life."

The vocabulary kids have these days!

" 'I can do all things through Christ who strengtheneth me' . . . and He's going to help me get up on skis today!"

I remembered her terror and resulting uncoordination the day before and gulped, "That's fine, honey; we'll try our best."

"No, Jesus will help me, I just know He will," was her determined reply. Some may call it correct psychological preparation, but I called it fulfilled faith as Jennifer skimmed along behind the boat shouting, "He did it! He did it! Thank You so much, Jesus!"

Involvement with children is full-time for those marrieds who have had several blessed events. For unmarrieds, there are usually many opportunities— from camps, Sunday School and neighbor's children to nieces and nephews.

One unmarried friend even adopted a cute little fellow—that's really involvement! When she first welcomed him into her home he was a frightened, neglected, abused child, stoically rejecting all gestures of affection. He has since been transformed into a bright, lovable and loving irresistible child— through the power of love!

The Elderly

Spending time with elderly friends can be equally enlightening and enjoyable. Medical science has done much to increase life expectancy but little has been done to increase life abundancy. Our society provides no useful role for these older citizens, and many of them exist in loneliness and depression with a feeling of worthlessness. Much of senility may be a psycho-emotional withdrawal from a hostile, unpleasant environment.

We can add much to the quality of the lives of our senior citizens by meaningful visits made with sincere interest. And, if we learn to listen, they will unfailingly enrich our lives as well. The seasoned wisdom of experience is unparalleled in our instant age of technology. Instead of carelessly tossing off the "yarns of

107

the old days," we may do well to listen. No historical reference can begin to give the depth of understanding of our heritage, with realistic feeling tones intact, as can these first-hand memories.

Some may argue that older people are not "with the times," and that their advice is obsolete. The aged may not understand or be able to accept some changes of the past few decades, but they still have an advantage. They've lived with people longer and basic human nature doesn't change.

Good relationships with older friends also help us to realistically face our own aging. Preparation shouldn't wait until the magical year of sixty-five, but should begin long before. We need to see aging as an achievement, not a disease. Paul, in 2 Corinthians 4:16 promises aging Christians, "Though our outward man is decaying, yet our inward man is renewed day by day." I shared that passage with an older friend recently and told her, "Why you're not getting older, you—the real you—are getting better!"

Youth usually avoids thinking about old age, just as they avoid the subject of death. We all need to face, to cope with and to accept the inevitability of both. And accepting old age is easier when we consider the finality of the alternative.

One of the loveliest, most gracious ladies I've ever known is presently enjoying her later years. She knew me as a child, in fact taught me Bible in the third grade. She provided a strong foundation of prayer that has supported me throughout my years, especially during crisis times. What a priceless treasure is her love and support. I'm very challenged to live and "finish well" with such beautiful grace as this dear lady, one of God's champions!

Marrieds/Unmarrieds

Socializing with people on the other side of the matrimonial fence is another means of expanding our life's perspective. The pleasures and pressures of both life-styles can be seen and appreciated. To be a comfortable experience, fraternizing with marrieds may require a solid sense of satisfaction with one's own present state of affairs. Also, it's good for us to understand that all is not "moonlight and roses" on either side of the honeymoon.

I see marital oneness as wonderful—I also see mately and parental responsibilities as exhausting. My married friends think my freedom is glorious— they also understand that my self-supporting efforts are at times lonely and hard. Close relationships with free, honest communication between marrieds and unmarrieds will help us to appreciate life's positives and realistically cope with its negatives.

Students

Another stage of life with which it is valuable to be compatible, if you've by chance survived it, is the student era. University students are often eager to find refuge from dorm bedlam. I remember as a student that my older, non-student friends helped to gear me from the pseudo-society of campus life. I know one Christian couple who entertains, with a scrumptious meal, between forty and fifty students a month in their home. Needless to say, they are loved and respected and their godly counsel is listened to.

Students also teach us much from their various fields of study, if we listen. And helping them with term papers or themes can be both an interesting and a giving experience.

Family

Perhaps the most important of our interpersonal relationships is that with our own nuclear family. Remember that, "Honor thy father and thy mother" is included in the Great Ten. The disintegration of the family unit is a dangerous sociological trend—no nation has survived it. It's also disastrous on an individual level.

We tend to lose sight that, as individuals, we are literally a part of our parents. Our original two cells joining to form new life, came from their bodies—our life-giving source. Not only genetically, but environmentally, our parents had untold influence in fashioning our attitudes, personalities and perspective.

To be severed from our heritage in our post-childhood years doesn't make sense. To be detached and distant from the lives who joined to produce and nurture our own isn't natural or right.

A good parent-child relationship should continue and the foundation of grateful love should be constant. A close bond of loving loyalty to our families in no way restricts our ability to "live our own lives." It rather gives us freedom to enjoy living in all of our relationships.

Without a strong family foundation, an individual may be severely hindered in all other interpersonal relationships. For example, if there is a lack of respect for our first authority—our parents, we will likely find it difficult to rightly react to other authorities in life. The habitual lawbreaker or insubordinate employee may have learned their disregard for authority early in life.

Men develop their concept of women from their mothers. Women think of men as they do their fathers. We develop patterns of reacting to the other sex in our parent-child relationship. Our whole emotional framework is built during those years and is not suddenly transformed by the "ideal mate."

Unresolved conflicts with parents indicate future conflicts within self and with spouse. Smoldering resentment may be quickly kindled by any minor irritation. Such responses as, "You're just like my nagging mother" or "You're just as inconsiderate as my father," are likely.

Unresolved conflict can also cause a reoccurrence of the same thing in our own lives. Resentment becomes such an integral part of our background that we become guilty of the same fault. Jacob was caught in this trap.

In his childhood, Jacob was very aware that his father, Isaac, favored his brother Esau. He deceived his way into an undeserved blessing and barely escaped Esau's anger with his neck intact— not exactly a picture of "Family of the Year."

Then later Jacob himself became the victim of deception and acquired more wives than he bargained for as the result. Finally, after much hard work and a bad case of mistaken identity, he started a family of his own.

But guess what caused most of his family feuds! Favoritism! His older sons sold poor favorite Joseph down the River Nile to be a slave in the land of Egypt. The story ends happily, but not before a great deal of pain was caused because father Jacob repeated the mistake of his father Isaac.

Is it ever possible to resolve these conflicts of bitterness and resentment? Yes, for resolution is basically within ourselves, in our attitudes. Our attitudes can be converted from bitterness, rebelliousness and pride to loving gratefulness.

Most parents will readily respond to genuine, humble effort to release tension and restore unity. A completely restored relationship may not be possible. But neither is a sincere "Will you forgive me?" likely to be rejected.

I have mentioned my own family throughout these chapters, for I can't discuss life without them. I'm unable to express my heart of thankfulness as I understand more of God's grace in giving me a loving home. It was so natural for me to respond to God's love for I experienced it in the quality of my parents' love.

Although I've left home, my parents are still a source of wise counsel and support with their unconditional love. They are not possessive, but encourage my independence and initiative. I say with David, "The lines are fallen unto me in pleasant places; Yea, I have a godly heritage" (Ps. 16:6, *KJV*).

I'm also sobered in the knowledge that "to whomsoever much is given, of him shall be much required" (Luke 12:48, *KJV*). I've known exceeding much and am far from the "required much." I pray that I will be faithful in fulfilling what God has started. If such a heritage is yours be thankful and sober with me.

God isn't unfaithful to those who have no such a background. A non-Christian home is never His desire, yet He can make use of such a setting to develop special insight and sensitivities. A good friend, who has her own happy family now, came from one of the worst situations I've ever known. Multiple divorce, alcohol and crime robbed her of any outward means of security. Through it all, God refined her into one of His most beautiful jewels. Her kind, wise spirit is radiant. She can identify with human suffering and need with unique understanding, and shares with authority God's sufficiency.

God wants to bring tremendous depth into parent-child relationships, even if parents are non-Christian. "Honor thy father and thy mother" isn't followed by the qualification "if they happen to be godly." Not only do we prevent future conflicts for ourselves by obeying this command but our obedience and respect may have eternal effects on unbelieving parents. An appreciative, respectful child will be heard at the soul level!

The Art of Closed Mouth, Open Heart

Social interaction need not always be a loud, outgoing noisy process. Perhaps the most significant of all contact is that of the quiet moments of listening. Ethel Barrett tells us not only to listen to what another is saying, but to listen to what is not being said.[2] That takes practice and the extreme discipline of keeping our own mouths shut.

Listening is evidence that we care enough to hear what is important to another, more than we want to explain what is important to us. Too often we're only interested in impressing others with our own bright thoughts, our vast wealth of knowlede. We're anxious to give advice when we haven't taken the time to discern the problem. Listening is an art, and those who are well-accomplished are valued friends.

Another art, that of being hospitable, is also a prerequisite if we are to reach God's highest in the area of sociability. This art isn't learned by party-giving or etiquette-keeping. Hospitality is far more than a specific act; it's an attitude, a receptivity of spirit that warmly welcomes all.

The workshop of hospitality is the home. Our homes are expressions of ourselves, and should reflect a place where we are comfortable and eager to receive guests, expected or not. Such homes are not kept without effort. A messy, disorganized home doesn't speak well of the rest of our lives and is certainly not welcoming to visitors. Friends, all shapes and sizes, should feel welcome to come and leave feeling refreshed. An atmosphere of relaxed host- or hostess-ship invites them to return soon and often.

I learned much of the true spirit and art of hospitality during a recent trip to some of the West Indies islands. I had the unforgettable privilege of worshiping with a rural congregation in Haiti and afterward eating Sunday dinner at the home of the native pastor. That small mud home, with thatched roof and dirt floors, was a palace in terms of the welcome I received.

The pastor stood with a clean towel and small basin of clear water with a cordial invitation to freshen up before dinner. I marveled at the fresh white tablecloth on the small table, heaped with delicious native food. Even without common race or language we shared a rare bond of fellowship as we thanked God for His provision around that small table. My smiling muscles haven't been the same since.

After lunch I walked several miles with these new friends before boarding the jeep that took me back to the mission compound. A lovely 15-year-old girl named Rosa shyly approached me and stopped to wipe my dusty shoes as I turned to leave. Deeply moved, I felt as if Jesus Himself had kneeled to wash my feet. Rosa reflected His character of unselfish, giving-love in a way I have never known. As I reluctantly hugged her goodby, it was with joyful assurance that we would have another visit someday—an eternal one without language barriers. I'm looking forward to that!

No, people-bumping isn't easy, but it's well worth the effort. The process—whether it be with peers, children, the elderly, students, marrieds, unmarrieds, family—the process develops either character or cynicism. Cynicism denies love—strong character demands it!

Footnotes

1. Ethel Barrett, "Advice to People Bumpers," *Family Life Today*, Vol. I, No. 1 (Dec. 1974), p. 8. © Copyright 1975 by Gospel Light Publications, Glendale, Ca. 91209.
2. Ethel Barret, *op cit.*, p. 10.

NINE
MENTAL DEVELOPMENT: STRETCH YOUR NEURONS

How mentally "fit" are you? Does your gray matter get enough exercise to be conditioned for real action? Or, are your neurons settling back in overstuffed easy-chairs, hibernating in comfortable laziness? We fail to stretch our minds, to expand our understanding. It's so much easier to stay in our nice, undemanding grooves of knowing just enough to exist. Reaching toward our mental potential doesn't require enrolling in a Ph.D. program—it's by no means confined to the academic world.

A good fitness program for the mind includes development of talents, creativity, interests, and enlarging our general knowledge and world view. There are all sorts of challenging directions in which to venture if only we would start moving our minds. Perhaps the most important place to check for mental cobwebs is in our vocations.

Economics require that most of us specialize in a chosen field, spend time in studying and practice, then occupy that occupation. In other words, we have to "make a living."

That process of making is, for some, a tiresome, boring or exhausting effort. The weekly paycheck is the only reward and often it's too meager to bring much consolation. For others, the making is a challenging task to be enjoyed, not endured. Payday is a result, not a goal.

The difference isn't in the vocation but in the mind-set of each individual. No job should be just a bread-winning gimmick, but should include vision and purpose. That vision comes as we choose our vocation—a task that seems to baffle many, because it involves the even more baffling business of knowing God's will.

You *Are* God's Will

"How do I find God's will?" is a question that literally haunts many in fear that they will miss "The Plan" and be doomed forever. A pastor, Rev. Roy Putnam, who has greatly influenced my life over the past five years, used this illustration that humorously portrays our mistaken concept of guidance:

"We think of God as the great Easter Bunny, hiding His will in brightly colored eggs. He watches as we hunt for them, remarking 'You're hot' or 'You're cold,' as we approach the hidden spot.

"Or we picture Him sadistically plotting to make us miserable. He looks down to the athlete and says, 'I know what I'll do. I'll break both of his legs and make him play the flute.' Or He looks to the bachelor and says . . . 'I know what I'll do . . . I'll give him a

117

woman he can't live with, and then I'll really fix him, I'll give him six younguns!' "

We smile, but can we recognize these fallacies in our own thinking? God wants to give us His best, His highest, but we continue to cringe in doubt that we can "find it" or, when we do, whether we will be able to endure it.

We don't have to stumble along some foggy path in desperation for a package labeled and dated, "God's will for Bill: issued July 4, void July 5." Those who imagine that they find such a package with a "Whew, I'm glad that's over with!" will surely be disillusioned and at a loss when any unexpected change comes in the course of living. Nor should we dread it as some crushing ton that will miserably obliterate us—you know, "Please God, don't make me a missionary to Africa—I hate snakes." God's ways and thoughts are so much higher than ours, and His will for us is far greater than our fearful-package mentality.

The whole key to assurance in the midst of God's purposes is to realize that, as obedient heirs, we *are* His will. We do not have to find God's will; we can be living in it daily.

Much Scripture that is frequently used in terms of specific subjective guidance, speaks in context of obedience to God's commands. If we neglect to obey His will we will never reach His highest in vocation or anything else.

Perhaps the most familiar of these passages is Proverbs 3:5,6. By reading these verses in context, we can see that their focus goes beyond a specific situation to a larger life thrust.

Proverbs 3:1-6 begins with:

"Let thy heart keep my commandments" with the result . . . "length of days and years of life, and peace will they add to thee" (*ASV*).

"Let not kindness and truth (or love and wisdom!) forsake thee" with the result . . . "so shalt thou find favor and good repute in the sight of God and man."

These verses deal with the whole continuum of life. Now verses five and six:

"Trust in Jehovah with all thy heart and lean not upon thine own understanding. In all thy ways acknowledge Him . . . ."

or paraphrased,

"We are limited with our finite minds in our understanding of an infinite God and His world. But we can, by faith, trust His goodness and love with all our being . . . and seek to please Him in everything we do."

The result of such a heart-attitude and mind-set is in the last portion of verse six:

"And He will direct, or make straight, our paths."

or paraphrased

"God will honor our trust by continuing His creative work in us as we develop into all that He intended us to be."

This process requires that we follow instructions—choose obedience and reject disobedience. This doesn't negate the need for specific direction on certain occasions, nor the desire of God to provide it. But it does define the relationship that is necessary before we can tune in to the specific desires of God for our individual lives.

The prayer of our hearts must be, as it was for Jesus, "Not my will, but thine be done" (Luke 22:42, *KJV*). Our one thrust, our one objective in life, must be to please God. Only then can we have a solid foundation of confidence that God is sovereign in the whole of our lives—that He is "directing our paths," our decisions and choices.

Such a life is not without failures—but it can be without despair that the "way" has been missed. "A man's goings are established of Jehovah; and he delighteth in his way. Though he fall, he shall not be utterly cast down, for Jehovah upholdeth him with his hand" (Ps. 37:23,24, *ASV*).

Rooted Wills and Productive Minds

So how does all this provide practical help in choosing a vocation or making any other important decisions in life? Simply this: as our wills are deeply rooted in the fertile soil of a Higher Will, our minds will become productive in wisely choosing the best. His Spirit within us directs this process. We have climbed up and are seeing life from God's perspective; we can now better discern our place of significance in the movement of life.

We need to remember that much of godly discernment is simply "sanctified" common sense. Consider: (1) if God created us as individuals, then we are special and unique; (2) if we have been restored back into His family as obedient heirs, then we *are* His will. Logically then, our inner inclinations are necessarily part of His will. Therefore, our individual preferences, tendencies and talents should be a major consideration in choosing our vocation.

As one of God's unique creations, and as a part of His will, discern that environment which is most natural for you, which allows you to fulfill your potential as an individual and which permits God to bring to

120

maturity those certain abilities and sensitivities that He has given you to accomplish His purposes in the world.

A prayer that I learned many years ago seems applicable here. It's not "God, use me," but "Lord, make me usable." As our inner capacity matures, so our outward effectiveness expands. Demonstrative action in serving God with an exciting ministry on all levels of human need is an inevitable outgrowth of inner wealth.

Apply these guidelines to your study or work situation:

Does it give you valuable understanding of yourself and others?

Does it help reinforce God-given positives and discourage unwanted traits?

Does it develop worthwhile talents and qualities?

Does it provide a climate in which you are to "be usable" in God's program for His world?

Does it challenge you to depend on God's sufficiency, or do you feel completely capable, sometimes even bored?

The most rewarding experiences are often those we enter into with fear and trepidation. "Going out on a limb" with limits of practical sensibility is great as long as we know that we are not alone.

Choose experiences which will have the most positive long-range results for you and others. Develop life goals as you begin to understand God's heart for you and His world. See your occupation in terms of reaching these goals.

"But it's too late for me to change occupations," you protest.

It's *never* too late, but be sure it's the job—and not

you— that needs changing before you reverse directions. Dissatisfaction, unfulfillment and lack of outreach may be due to your mind-set, not your job. Frustrations, tension and fatigue are inherent in any vocation—as in life itself.

At the same time, there are few, if any, fields that are boring and unfulfilling when a person is striving toward being the best he can be in that field. Being the best takes discipline, hard work and motives higher than the purely monetary, yet the overall feeling of accomplishment is worth it!

Brain Strain

Mental stretching can surely begin with our vocation. But we should not limit mental fitness to our own particular discipline. There's a lot of unknown territory waiting for our exploration. Whether our transportation be books, journals, films, lectures, television or formal classes—we can discover exciting new worlds by a disciplined effort to extend ourselves.

Here are a few observations and suggestions in basic areas to start your thinking:

History

Read history from the perspective of how God has been moving behind the scenes in the annals of time. An understanding of one's national heritage is important to clearly perceive the scope of present national conditions.

At the same time, a view of world history helps to pull us from national egocentricity of thinking. And it gives our view of world missions a completely fresh frame of reference.

Biographies and historical novels are two of my favorite sources of appreciation of past events and people.

English

Some of us are reluctant readers, perhaps because we are not comfortable with ourselves in quietness. Yet reading can be stimulating mental exercise, and certainly one of the best routes to broader horizons, spiritually and intellectually.

This is true, because literature is a combination of historical and philosophical trends, blended beautifully with human emotions. It's a revelation of inner worlds—of thoughts, of attitudes and moods written first in the soul and then on paper.

There's such a vast collection of good works from which to choose. Suit your own tastes and moods—but at least delve into some of the world's great writing, and you'll soon find your own preferences.

And try your hand at writing! Letters are a great place to begin developing your ability to express yourself.

"Dear Diary" can be more than just an adolescent fad, too. Jim Elliot, one of the five martyred missionaries in the jungles of Ecuador, wrote his thoughts and feelings in a personal record, beginning with his college days. His profound observations now challenge many.

In any case, you will find the practice of writing will help you to solidify your own thinking on certain issues and to develop further insights into others.

Natural Science

There is absolutely no scientific data that is contrary to Scripture. Rather, there is only faulty inter-pretation by scientists with faulty presuppositions.

Science then is not the enemy of Christianity, any more than reason is the enemy of faith. As Alfred North Whitehead stated in citing the original premise of early science: since the world was created by a reasonable God, it can be understood by reason. From this premise came the scientific method.

Within a Christian frame of reference, it's exciting to discover how natural laws and order reveal much about the Designer of this world. Modern science, a vast collection of facts and theories that surround and touch the core of life, has yet been unable to define it. But as Christians, we know the "spark of life" is not an unknown variable—we know its Source.

To us then as Christians, the study of scientific data should have even greater significance than to others. And what better way than through the study of science to begin understanding ourselves and our universe. Begin with the many uncomplicated, non-technical books available in all the sciences. Then go on to develop some hobbies from science, such as gardening, astronomy, bird-watching, etc.

Social Science

In recent years, Christians have invaded and gained prominence in the social sciences, an area of study that can give us valuable information as to the inner mechanisms of reasoning and personality.

For example, anyone working in a foreign culture should have some exposure to anthropology. And we can all gain new appreciation for the complexity of human personality, both individual and collective, from the study of psychology and sociology.

Such study can help us see some of the cause and effect relationships in our mental-emotional life, such as guilt turning to depression, or the influences of heredity and environment on mental stability.

Two cautions: (1) Avoid the dangerous trend of taking no responsibility for personal problems, blaming them entirely on some past trauma. God does hold us responsible and offers a sure cure for guilt. (2) Don't get caught in the trap of deep introspection and self-analysis. Better not overdo analysis of others either!

Fine Arts (music, art, and drama)

Whether it be participating or appreciating, there's a tremendous reservoir of possibilities in the area of the fine arts. Art can take many forms: painting, sketching or sculpturing, for instance. Crafts can be included too—knitting, woodworking, glassblowing, jewelry-making, carving, macrame, decoupage, even flower-arranging.

Results may not be professional or even appropriate for public exposure, but it's fun to find and enjoy an outlet for your own personal creativity. It's a God-given gift, being creative, and needs practice to develop.

The world of music is another area of creativity and offers something for everyone's preference. Participate if possible, but definitely learn to appreciate. Study the lives of artists and composers; compare their life philosophies with their works, where moods and obsessions often take nonverbal forms.

Political Science (current events)

Jesus was well aware of the political and social

system of His day with all its attendant problems. And Christians today should be no less aware of the times in which they live. Keeping abreast of current events is not just a pastime for politically minded men—it should be a prerogative of every concerned citizen.

Informative sources include newspapers, television and journals. In many communities, there are also discussion groups, forums and seminars that are open to the public. And informal discussions of issues and events with others help you to broaden your knowledge and to gain further understanding.

The "signs of the times" are becoming more visible today, especially through the nation of Israel. So a good book on prophecy may be the best source yet on current events!

Economics

Not many of us have the answer to inflation, but we should have sufficient economic background to regulate our personal finances. Good budget practices are part of the command to be good stewards.

Many marriages suffer over money-related disagreements. These might be solved through some basic knowledge of budgeting and a large dose of unselfishness. The unmarried, without the financial responsibilities of a family, have all sorts of creative avenues to use money wisely.

Affluence isn't sinful, and poverty isn't spiritual! As Paul wrote in Philippians 4:11 (*NASB*), we all must learn how "to be content in whatever circumstances." So it's not how much we have that's important, but how we use it and how we feel about it that counts.

You may need to examine your money-mind. If dollar signs cloud your vision, shift your values and re-order your priorities. And keep a budget!

Be wise in finances, but more importantly find the secret Paul found: "to be content in whatever."

Sports

The "wide world of sports" gives us a multitude of participant and spectator sports from which to choose. Such activities not only promote our physical development, but also exercise our minds, broaden our interests and develop our character. Controlled tempers, humility and honesty may best be learned in the arena.

Always be ready to try something new. Hiking, snow and water skiing, biking, sailing, flying, swimming, horseback riding, jogging, scuba and skin diving, and surfing are only a few possibilities that are usually non-competitive.

Tennis, golf, hockey, football, basketball, soccer, baseball, track, gymnastics, Ping-Pong and chess are a few other possibilities for friendly competition.

Why don't you try at least one from each list as a new project this month?

Travel

Travel is the best education you can buy! Like history, travel broadens our world view and narrows our national egocentricity. It may also initiate foreign language study and give real meaning to our knowledge of geography.

Don't just go somewhere to see the sights—observe the people beyond the monuments. Get to know the people and listen to what they are saying.

International friendships developed during travel are the highlight of any trip and will be long remembered and treasured.

To hear of economic and spiritual poverty is one thing; to see and meet world-wide need in living color is quite another thing—an unforgettable reality.

These suggestions are by no means exhaustive. Let your mental exercise be as individual as you are. Set priorities and dig in.

God's Filter for Our Minds

But be selective in the things to which you expose your mind. The Bible sets some pretty high standards here:

"Whatever is worthy of reverence and is honorable and seemly, whatever is just, whatever is pure, whatever is lovely and lovable, whatever is kind and winsome and gracious, if there is any virtue and excellence, if there is anything worthy of praise, think on and weigh and take account of these things—fix your minds on them" (Phil. 4:8, *Amplified*).

So examine what you are feeding your mind and see if it meets God's standards. Scripture doesn't eliminate sin and evil from its inspired account of life. But it unfailingly portrays evil in its ugliness, and good as the best, most rewarding choice. Evaluate the last book you read, the last movie you saw by God's criteria.

Mental exercise takes discipline and effort, but it can be fun and is certainly rewarding. A fresh mental outlook as a result of spring-cleaning the settled, dusty ruts may be the best medicine in the world for the "blahs."

Look back over the last five chapters and set some

specific goals for yourself in each of the areas: physical, sexual, emotional, social and mental. Be realistic —but also expectantly enthused. Whether it be a low calorie diet, a book on Slobovian culture, or a trip to an old folks' home—see your goals as means to a higher end: to please God in every area of living.

But let's not get up the creek without a paddle. We've been talking about getting into the mainstream of life. But a canoe on the loose without an instrument of power or control and with no direction will end either splintered on the rocks or marooned on the shore. We have a Source of power, a direction, and control available—all we have to do is follow instructions!

TEN
SPIRITUAL DEVELOPMENT: WHEN ALL ELSE FAILS, FOLLOW INSTRUCTIONS

You're an individual, married or not! That's God's perspective of you. As He looks at you He sees His own special creation, unique from any other, one that He loves more than His life. You are as important to Him as if you were the only person on earth.

Heaven isn't some complex control center that reduces us to "don't bend, fold, or mutilate" impersonals. Our needs aren't categorized and given some premixed solution or stock prescription. We aren't sent to a secretarial Archangel in room 304 to fill out forms and wait for an appointment with the special agent of our local, earthly district.

The Bible gives the real picture of our significance in the heavenlies. "For the eyes of the Lord move to and fro throughout the earth that He may strongly support those whose heart is completely His" (2 Chron. 16:9, *NASB*).

Not only is God always available to meet us on an individual basis, but He is actively pursuing the opportunity to "strongly support" us. As we, with wonder, grasp this concept of God's perspective of us, we

130

will surely change our view of God, of ourselves, of others and of life in general.

God wants to give each unique individual more than an "I'm happy . . . , I guess" existence. He wants to provide a life that is higher than a status quo humdrum. So He gives instructions on "how we can be all we are meant to be."

Operation Restoration

The first instruction for putting together God's highest life for us is to meet the conditional phrase in the verse we just quoted, "those whose heart is completely His."

How do our hearts become completely God's?

By responding to God's demonstrated love in repentance of personal rebellion. This response, if genuine, will produce a life that has one motivating thrust; a one-track life consistently God-conscious in all areas of personal development. That one objective —to please God—infiltrates every dimension of such a life: physical, sexual, emotional, social, mental, spiritual.

An increase of God-consciousness, or spiritual growth, can only be accomplished in the mainstream of living, only as we bring every part of ourselves in line with God's standards on an everyday basis. So, the essential environment for spiritual development is letting God's standards permeate every aspect of our lives. Then, and *only* then, will we be healthy, integrated, total persons.

Reaching toward our individual human potential is not an egotistical self-improvement plan. Rather, it's the progressive development of godly character in each unique personality, the fulfillment of all we were meant to be. God calls this total development "holiness." This is not a halo-surrounded super piety, but a practical everyday reality.

Dr. J. Sidlow Baxter, one of my favorite Bible expositors, says this of holiness:

"Holiness is restoration—the restoring of our nature to its true humanhood. It is not a never-ending crucifixion of human self, but a renewing of it. Neither is it a grinding suppression of what we naturally are, but the purifying and renovating of it into the image of Jesus.

"Regeneration reaches into the whole human personality. It diffuses its healthful new life through every part. . . . Regeneration quickens, and inwrought holiness fulfills, all that is truest and best in what we are by the very essence of our nature as human beings. (Remember, we're made in the image of God.)

"Holiness is not a foreign country, it is the prodigal coming home, to live where he really belongs."[1]

The process of holiness isn't through our self-effort. It is the renewing and restoring work of the Holy Spirit within our spirit, as we give Him access to all our being.

Dr. Baxter contrasts this concept with the familiar "victorious life" teaching:

"According to it, the Christian life is not lived by the believer at all, but by Christ Himself in and through the believer. . . . Actually that is no 'victorious life' at all. No, for Christ has supplanted me. He is the actor of my actions. There is absolutely no education or development of my own character. Christian holiness is the *true* man—the renewed, restored, completed human character, after the image of the Lord Jesus.[2]

With the realization that it *is* God's work in "educating" our character, we are not deceived that it is our own efforts of doing good. But we can become excited about the tremendous potential within each of us to be restored, to be the best we can be.

Operation Communication

We've been talking about the demonstrative *milieu* of spiritual development. Now, let's affirm the basic *means* of such God-consciousness. We cannot increase or develop that which we do not have. Knowing God, His guidelines and the process of obedience doesn't come by osmosis. Spirituality must be resident before it can be demonstrated.

We are living in the age of the immediate, the era of the instant. We want things to happen fast and happen now. Industry gives us instant products, drugs give us instant highs, computers give us instant data, jets give us instant travel and satellites give us instant world media.

We are developing an overall expectancy that anticipates and demands instant fulfillment, or none at all. We become frustrated with any process that is long and tedious. Our boiling points are lowering and our range of tolerance is decreasing.

This tendency to expect the instantaneous also affects our perspective of spirituality. "What we are" and "what we know we should be" are too far apart. We want five easy steps, a secret formula, a novel approach, a spectacular experience—anything that will bridge that gap *now* and once for all. In short, we want instant spirituality, instant holiness.

133

But God's Word tells us that He desires a solid, personal relationship with each one of us that is progressively deepened by close communication. His process may be a slower, more gradual, day-by-day refining—but it is far more satisfying than a burst of emotional ecstasy. Such rapture certainly has its place in our relationship with God, but emotions cannot be our sole spiritual thermometer.

Our relationship with God will be shallow without communication on a daily basis. Prayer then is much more than a spiritual exercise, a Christian duty, a pious ritual. It is direct, personal, intimate communication, the very breath of our faith. It is a command— a loving call to meet God heart to heart everyday. And we do not have to understand prayer, only obey and enjoy.

O. Hallesby's book called *Prayer* gives much insight into the beauty of such communication. Hallesby terms prayer as "coupling the powers of heaven to our helplessness." It's not necessary for us to go through spiritual gymnastics when we pray, or soul exertion that will make an impression upon God.[3]

In prayer, we come to God and share with Him our desires, as we do with anyone whom we love and who loves us. We don't have to agonize to help God find a solution to our problems—we just present our needs with confidence in a loving Father.

At times, prayer becomes conversation with God in the midst of daily work and activities. I often pray in the elevator on the way to my office. I love to talk to God when I'm horseback riding, one of my favorite activities. There's no more natural place to praise God than in the fields and woods.

God desires our thanks; His heart of love is so

tender to our receptivity of His goodness to us. Hallesby comments, "We have been created to give glory to God—every time we do so, we are in harmony with His plans and purposes for our lives."[4] Praise feels good to us and to God!

Sometimes our communication with God is without words, "as we rest our weary souls in quiet contemplation of Him." Hallesby describes such times, "We, too, become tired, deathly tired, of ourselves, of others, of the world, of life, of everything!

"It is blessed to know of a place where we can lay our tired head and hearts, in our heavenly Father's arms, and say to Him, 'I can do no more. And I have nothing to tell you. May I lie here a while and rest?' "[5]

I remember such an evening when all of life seemed black, and I became deeply disturbed that I could not pray. Too weary to do anything but cry, I went to bed and wept in lonely frustration. My mother came in, asked what was the matter and, after ascertaining my momentary weakness of body and spirit, gave me this wise, gentle bit of advice: "Honey, you don't have to pray with words. Just lie there and let God love you."

How comforting that was and what a sense of close fellowship I experienced in the knowledge of God's unconditional love and presence.

Don't misunderstand—we shouldn't always just "lie there" every time we don't particularly feel like praying. It's the exception rather than the rule.

Prayer is an exciting, privileged communication with the God of the universe, but it's also exacting work requiring disciplined effort.

Why?

Because, as Jesus instructed, we are to pray "in

secret," not on the street corner for all to see our outstanding performances. We lose much motivation to pray because it is not seen and openly appreciated. As Hallesby explains, "It is astonishing to see how much it means to have others see what we do. The fact that our work is appreciated and valued is a remarkable stimulant to us."[6]

Satan knows this proud tendency in our lives and uses prayerlessness as the most subtle, "the most painless way of stealing from us our spiritual life."[7] We need to rebuke fiercely this thief and ask for help from the Holy Spirit who is already praying for and with us. (See Rom. 8:26,27, *KJV*).

Just as God communicates with us in prayer, so He also communicates with us in His objective Word. Remember, we need to know His instructions before we can follow them. A little-people friend of mine, at the age of five, stated this so profoundly. She approached her dad with this proposal, "Daddy, can we read the Bible too, not just my Bible storybook? I need to know what God says to do and not to do, so that I can obey Him."

Consider a driver stubbornly refusing to read a driver's manual before driving. The driver may carry the manual with him, in fact, keep it on the seat right beside him. But as he approaches and intersection and desperately searches the index for appropriate action . . . crunch!! Too late!

Aren't we just as foolish to neglect study of our life manual until a crisis situation is impending? The "crunch" may not be too comfortable, but of even greater concern is the fact that we have disappointed

136

the One who wants so much to communicate with us, to "strongly support" us! The Bible is His communication, not only to the world in a general sense, but to *you* personally in the singular and present tense.

Why do we neglect it? Much for the same reasons we do prayer. We place our priorities on outward evidences of our spirituality, on how much we can do. We need to realize that we will suffer inner poverty through lack of communication with our Power Source which will, in turn, make our most generous efforts meaningless.

God wants us . . . not our activity.

The methods of communication with God can be just as individual as we are. Many types of study have been outlined, many forms of prayer have been suggested. What's important is that we seek honest, open communication, with regular times of quietness to discern the often "still, small voice of God."

Sing Scripture, pray hymns, study biblical topics, memorize passages, pray in words of Scripture—completely saturate your thinking with the truths of God. Other books, both devotional and informatively apologetic, can complement Scripture and prayer, but can *never* substitute. Read widely of the tremendous resources from godly writers but let your foundation of truth be the inspired Word.

Our communication with God isn't to be a monastic, isolating practice in utter solitude. Times alone are vitally important and should be a disciplined effort. But we mature largely as our communication becomes a natural part of all of our hours. God uses many circumstances and experiences to make His Word a part of us.

We need to become flexible, to become sensitive in

choosing experiences that will integrate God's truth in our lives. My learning times range from teaching a Bible study, or listening to lectures of highly intellectual apologetics, or counseling an unwed mother, or dealing with an attempted suicide . . . to chasing a snake from my cabin at camp!

God makes truth real to us as we involve ourselves in life and in others. It's a wonderful process, full of surprises!

Without a close relationship of communication with God, all that we've explored together is meaningless. Without being close enough to climb into higher arms we cannot see life from a different perspective. Without spending time with God we cannot have a clear concept of Him. Without experiencing daily acceptance into His presence, we will not know how to fully accept ourselves and others. Without communication we cannot please God and our life loses its basic thrust.

In contrast, the communicating Christian has a solid foundation on which the rest of his life is built. He has a sense of purposeful personal integration; all the forces within and without his person blend together to produce holiness, or life at its best. He experiences the fulfillment of this oft-repeated prayer, "O God, make me intensely spiritual but keep me perfectly natural and always thoroughly practical —even as Jesus was."

Such a person is not only communicating with God—he is communicating with his world. He is most effective in proclaiming truth as he consistently reflects the character of God. He verbally affirms the Source of that higher quality of living and challenges others, by his words and life, to seek that Source.

It is our fulfillment to share our faith, not just our commission. Seeing new life capture the heart of another, as a result of our sharing, is an unparalleled privilege that reaffirms and refreshes our own faith. Such sharing may come best in the natural give-and-take relationships in the midst of everyday living.

And remember, Jesus met whole people, not just souls, and accepted them as they were before He transformed their total beings. His reflected character in us requires the same giving, unconditional love and concern for the total man. He has entrusted the task of revealing Himself to us and through us. What a responsibility and joy!

Only the Beginning

God wants to provide the richest life possible for each individual one of us. This new perspective of life gives us purpose, expectancy and fulfillment. It does *not* rid life of all problems and pain, of all failure. Let's face it: life is often hard, frustrating, disappointing, if not utterly exhausting.

Although God does not free us from problems, He does bring to life an inner richness that helps us cope with problems without despair. He does not guarantee us automatic, fulltime happiness, but He can assure progressively deepening contentment that infuses into the far, dark corners of our hearts where happiness never quite reaches.

Such contentment rejects a bored, pessimistic restlessness or resignation of, "Oh, well, it could be worse!" Such contentment is, at times, a quiet enthusiasm of spirit—at other times it takes the face of joyous exuberancy.

Whatever form, contentment is a positive attitude

139

toward every day that cannot help but be contagious. It's rooted in the deep satisfaction of belonging to and pleasing God—a God who is perfectly good and loving.

The little, hard-to-find book of Habakkuk—chapter 3, verses seventeen through nineteen, slightly paraphrased—closes with this same positive attitude, a joyful awareness of the privilege that is uniquely ours of living a fulfilling God-conscious, God-pleasing life.

"Though the kids be cranky,
    and I haven't had much sleep for three weeks,
Though my job application was turned down,
    and my rent has gone up twice,
Though the car broke down,
    and it was 101 degrees in the shade,
Though the one I love most failed me,
    and blames me for the hurt,
"Yet I will rejoice in Jehovah
I will joy in the God of my salvation.
Jehovah, the Lord, is my strength;
    And He maketh my feet like hinds' feet
And will make me to walk upon my high
    places" (*ASV*).

Footnotes

1. J. Sidlow Baxter, *A New Call to Holiness* (Grand Rapids, Michigan: Zondervan Publishing House, 1973), pp. 123-125.
2. J. Sidlow Baxter, *op. cit.*, p. 118,119,124.
3. O. Hallesby, *Prayer*. Augsburg Publishing House. Used by permission.
4. *Ibid.*, p. 139.
5. *Ibid.* p. 148.
6. *Ibid.* p. 163.
7. *Ibid.* p. 87.